Destination ... CHANGE

JOURNEY TO EMPOWERMENT

Brenda Jones

iUniverse, Inc.
Bloomington

Destination ... CHANGE
JOURNEY TO EMPOWERMENT

iUniverse books may be ordered through booksellers or by contacting:

iUniverse
1663 Liberty Drive
Bloomington, IN 47403
www.iuniverse.com
1-800-Authors (1-800-288-4677)

ISBN: 978-1-4502-8275-8 (sc)
ISBN: 978-1-4502-8276-5 (ebook)

Printed in the United States of America

iUniverse rev. date: 01/18/2011

DEDICATIONS

To my son, Marcus, the star that lights up my world. You never gave up on me and you loved me unconditionally. This book is for you, in honor of your greatness as a father, son and most important – as a man. Never forget that God has chosen you to lead the way.

To my brother, Larry, a man of honor who has been supportive through my dark days. You are always there with solutions, giving me the hope and the courage to go on. Our "spirits" will forever be connected.

To my father, Lawrence … you have always been my hero through the good and the bad. My dreams as a little girl were to someday make you proud. I thank God for accomplishing that before you were taken to your final resting place. The only thing more powerful than a daughter's devotion is her father's love. In honor of you, Daddy … my "Quiet Storm".

Acknowledgements

I thank God first and foremost for the opportunity to be His vessel, in carrying out the message of hope, unity and courage.

"Forever Free" program in Chino, for providing "a way out" to women who are lost, as I once was. Thank you for giving me a life beyond my wildest dreams.

Linda Burns Hervey, for believing in me during a time when I couldn't believe in myself, while looking past the women in "blue".

Mildred Jenkins, for always being the calm spirit of constant guidance in the midst of my life's many storms.

Deanna Moody-Kivett, for your unwavering friendship and authenticity. When others change, you remain consistent and 'real'.

Lapreal Miller – you are my kindred spirit, who has inspired me daily by your example to be better than yesterday.

Special thanks to Rhea, who gave me the vision and concept for Part I of this book. Sangita, Brianna, Rebecca Y. and Audra – your support and encouragement have been priceless. Sandy L. – you were the catalyst God spoke through in order to take me to a much higher ground than I ever imagined. To Suzi Reynolds, for her expertise and diligence in typing and organizing my manuscript with love. I couldn't have done it without you. God bless you all!

AUTHOR'S NOTE

My journey of addiction took me to many dark places filled with despair and demoralization. This journey included a lot of county jail time, finally resulting in my first, but not my last term in state prison (two more terms followed). With no drugs or freedom for a long time, I was left with my thoughts and emotions that had been numbed from years of chemical abuse and the lifestyle that went with it. While in the receiving facility at the California Institution for Women (CIW), these feelings began to emerge. God intervened, as he had done so many times in my addiction with a way out ... poetry. These poems began my quest of healing and obtaining clarity. I continued to write for the first two years, as I embarked on building a foundation of recovery. This outlet allowed me to clear out some wreckage of my past, which opened the door for God to guide and direct my path to the life I have today, a grateful, recovering addict/alcoholic, with 18 years of sobriety. This gift of recovery has given me the opportunity to work in the mental health profession as a substance abuse counselor. My purpose is to help the lost souls find a way out of a life of self-destruction, while acquiring clarity on "Self" along the way.

Table of Contents

Part I: "Inside Me" (The Awakening)

Table of Contents (continued)

Part 1 "Inside Me" (The Awakening)

Part I

"Inside Me"

(The Awakening)

INTRODUCTION

(The Awakening)

Self-Awareness is developed through understanding our emotions as they relate to life's experiences. These feelings impact how we see ourselves and the choices we make. I hope this collection of simple poems with complex feelings enhances your perception of who you are as a person. Take advantage of the opportunity to process your innermost emotions provided by the journal questions. Find a safe, quiet place, grab a pen and embrace the journey .... "Inside Me".

"Inside Me"

Inside me is a woman wanting love and attention,
but past relationships brought bitter
apprehension.

Inside me lies a past of high hopes followed by
shattered dreams.

Drugs became my new hope as I lost all
self-esteem.

Inside me is the courage to walk through obstacles as they come;
feeling less than. I often sabotage the success and just run.

Inside me is a little girl broken, damaged by emotional neglect;
making choices as an adult, I created destruction and regrets.

A lot more than the naked eye can see,
if you really care, take time to look …

"Inside Me"

12/11/91

Written by:
Brenda Jones

<u>FOOD FOR THOUGHT</u>

The image we project is seldom indicative of the needs or desire related
to our inner being.

Journal Questions:

1) Explain the image you display to others in order to protect yourself. How does
   this image hinder your relationships?

_____

_____

_____

_____

_____

_____

_____

_____

_____

_____

_____

_____

_____

_____

_____

_____

_____

_____

_____

_____

_____

_____

_____

_____

_____

_____

_____

_____

_____

_____

_____

_____

2) Describe a situation that has left you apprehensive to trust again. How can you learn from these experiences in terms of how you choose who you trust?

_____
_____
_____
_____
_____
_____
_____
_____
_____
_____
_____
_____
_____
_____
_____
_____
_____
_____
_____
_____
_____
_____
_____
_____
_____
_____
_____
_____
_____
_____
_____
_____
_____
_____
_____
_____
_____

3) What do you want others to see when they look at you? How does your action send a much different message?

_____
_____
_____
_____
_____
_____
_____
_____
_____
_____
_____
_____
_____
_____
_____
_____
_____
_____
_____
_____
_____
_____
_____
_____
_____
_____
_____
_____
_____
_____
_____
_____

Look over your (3) journal questions and identify **_all_** your prominent issues in these situations. List them in the spaces below:

_____   _____   _____
_____   _____   _____
_____   _____   _____

Lesson:

Today, I honor the wholeness "Inside Me"

"Reflections"

Reflections escape through the corridors of my mind,
Memories joyous and painful are never left behind.

Filled with mirror images that are lasting and true,
Strength during the trying times will always shine through.

Reflections give me warm feelings inside,
Giving of myself no longer will I hide.

Understanding what isn't meant to be
quickly goes away, thanking God for coming
this far, each night, as I pray.

Reflections of the past can be good or bad.
I chose to grow from all the experiences I've had.

Life is a gamble, going in many different directions,
As I escape through corridors of my mind with …

Reflections
12/17/92

Written by:
Brenda Jones

FOOD FOR THOUGHT

Our perceptions of life's experiences has the power to defeat or
complete our destiny.

Journal Questions:

1) Describe a time in your life when happiness slipped away. How did that
experience teach you a valuable lesson?

_____

_____

_____

_____

_____

_____

_____

_____

_____

_____

_____

_____

_____

_____

_____

_____

_____

_____

_____

_____

_____

_____

_____

_____

_____

_____

_____

_____

_____

_____

_____

2) Explain one of your most painful experiences. How did it complete or defeat your development as a person?

_____
_____
_____
_____
_____
_____
_____
_____
_____
_____
_____
_____
_____
_____
_____
_____
_____
_____
_____
_____
_____
_____
_____
_____
_____
_____
_____
_____
_____
_____
_____
_____
_____
_____
_____
_____
_____
_____

3) How can you grow stronger because of adversities? List some situations where you persevered.

_____

_____

_____

_____

_____

_____

_____

_____

_____

_____

_____

_____

_____

_____

_____

_____

_____

_____

_____

_____

_____

_____

_____

_____

_____

_____

_____

_____

_____

_____

Look over your (3) journal questions and identify **_all_** your prominent issues in these situations. List them in the spaces below:

_____   _____   _____

_____   _____   _____

_____   _____   _____

Lesson:

My character is a positive "Reflection" of life's journeys.

"Inside Strong"

Escaping for protection to my child within,
But self-confidence is the message I tried to send.

From an early age, I retreated into my own world,
No love ever shown for that lonely little girl.

As a young adult, the world seemed cruel to me,
Rebellious I went in search of my own identity.

I couldn't seem to fit in with anyone, anywhere;
Eyes cold with empty hearts, no one really cared.

As a woman, I thought that love could be found in a man,
The wrong decision for myself, I didn't even understand.

That little girl, now a woman – through mistakes has grown,
Her protections while coping with life had become …

"Inside Strong"
12/29/92

Written by:
Brenda Jones

FOOD FOR THOUGHT

Who we are today is based on what we were taught yesterday.

Journal Questions:

1) Identify a coping skill you used as a child for protection. How has childhood vulnerability affected your development as an adult?

_____

_____

_____

_____

_____

_____

_____

_____

_____

_____

_____

_____

_____

_____

_____

_____

_____

_____

_____

_____

_____

_____

_____

_____

_____

_____

_____

_____

_____

_____

_____

_____

2) Have you ever isolated because of "fear of failing"? How did that fear affect your self-worth?

_____

_____

_____

_____

_____

_____

_____

_____

_____

_____

_____

_____

_____

_____

_____

_____

_____

_____

_____

_____

_____

_____

_____

_____

_____

_____

_____

_____

_____

_____

_____

_____

_____

_____

_____

_____

_____

_____

_____

_____

3) What kind of situations make you most uncomfortable? How can you take steps
to heal as an adult today?

_____

_____

_____

_____

_____

_____

_____

_____

_____

_____

_____

_____

_____

_____

_____

_____

_____

_____

_____

_____

_____

_____

_____

_____

_____

_____

_____

_____

_____

_____

_____

_____

Look over your (3) journal questions and identify **_all_** your prominent issues in
these situations. List them in the spaces below:

_____   _____   _____

_____   _____   _____

_____   _____   _____

Lesson:

I will not let my past dictate my future in a negative way.

"Shattered Dreams"

A comfortable home in which I have to live,
Quality time for my child, I wanted to give.

A life without drugs, attempts failed to stay clean,
Lost but not forgotten, now only shattered dreams.

Wanting to prove those wrong who ridiculed me,
Chains of my own persecution, I couldn't break free.

Searching to find what "love" really means,
Disappointment continued – followed by more shattered dreams.

I began to lose all faith, turning to the peace within,
Finding new hope; remembering God is my best friend.

Maybe now reflections of the past can be redeemed,
Becoming visions of the future, instead of only …

"Shattered Dreams"
1/11/93

Written by:
Brenda Jones

FOOD FOR THOUGHT

To focus on past failure increases the chance to repeat it.

Journal Questions:

1) What are some regrets you have regarding your life today? How has holding on to those memories hindered your progress?

_____

_____

_____

_____

_____

_____

_____

_____

_____

_____

_____

_____

_____

_____

_____

_____

_____

_____

_____

_____

_____

_____

_____

_____

_____

_____

_____

_____

_____

_____

_____

_____

_____

2) When did you start to truly believe in a power greater than yourself? How have your goals changed since recovery?

_____

_____

_____

_____

_____

_____

_____

_____

_____

_____

_____

_____

_____

_____

_____

_____

_____

_____

_____

_____

_____

_____

_____

_____

_____

_____

_____

_____

_____

_____

_____

_____

_____

_____

_____

3) Where do you see yourself in 5 years? How are you going to achieve these future dreams?

_____
_____
_____
_____
_____
_____
_____
_____
_____
_____
_____
_____
_____
_____
_____
_____
_____
_____
_____
_____
_____
_____
_____
_____
_____
_____
_____
_____
_____
_____
_____

Look over your (3) journal questions and identify **_all_** your prominent issues in these situations. List them in the spaces below:

_____   _____   _____
_____   _____   _____
_____   _____   _____

Lesson:

Today, I will create new dreams for old mistakes.

-20-

"Tears of Yesterday"

A struggle for perfection still does on inside,
Seeking understanding so my feelings can confide.

Inner strength an asset in coming this far,
Sometimes a liability in dealing with things as they are.

Confusion a part of my reflection on who I am,
Pain and sorrow haunt me, as I try to understand.

Past impressions invade corridors of my mind,
Causing doubt in myself from time to time.

A woman of tomorrow is the image I'd like to display,
As I continue to grow strong through …

"Tears of Yesterday"
2/8/93

Written by:
Brenda Jones

FOOD FOR THOUGHT

Focusing on all that is wrong blocks you from learning and
growing through the experience.

Journal Questions:

1) In what ways do you judge yourself by accomplishments of others? How has this behavior hampered your development?

_____
_____
_____
_____
_____
_____
_____
_____
_____
_____
_____
_____
_____
_____
_____
_____
_____
_____
_____
_____
_____
_____
_____
_____
_____
_____
_____
_____
_____
_____

2) When has doubt of your past decisions frozen you in fear? How has the need for perfection caused you negative outcome?

_____
_____
_____
_____
_____
_____
_____
_____
_____
_____
_____
_____
_____
_____
_____
_____
_____
_____
_____
_____
_____
_____
_____
_____
_____
_____
_____
_____
_____
_____
_____
_____
_____
_____
_____
_____
_____
_____
_____
_____

3) How has being too strong created a liability in your life? Describe a scenario where your strength helped you to endure?

_____
_____
_____
_____
_____
_____
_____
_____
_____
_____
_____
_____
_____
_____
_____
_____
_____
_____
_____
_____
_____
_____
_____
_____
_____
_____
_____
_____
_____

Look over your (3) journal questions and identify _**all**_ your prominent issues in these situations. List them in the spaces below:

_____   _____   _____
_____   _____   _____
_____   _____   _____

Lesson:

Tears of yesterday are healthy stepping stones to a successful tomorrow.

"Chances"

Chances in the fast lane I beat the odds,
Excitement of the moment I projected various facades.

Endangering my life and freedom I felt it was the only way,
Simply surviving, I became mentally exhausted day by day.

Chances to turn my life around I didn't take advantage of,
Desperately seeking understanding and an emotion called love …

Venturing anywhere I could, searching to no avail,
A dead end of self-destruction, constantly going to jail.

Chances of a positive nature if I stay on the right track,
A new life awaits me, never having to look back.

A happy ending to a story of one-sided romances,
Growing within, I can now beat the odds of …

"Chances"
1/14/93

Written by:
Brenda Jones

FOOD FOR THOUGHT

God gives us many chances. We must choose the path
that allows us to recover our losses.

Journal Questions:

1) What is your distinction between living and merely surviving? How did you
protect yourself in your disease against harm?

_____
_____
_____
_____
_____
_____
_____
_____
_____
_____
_____
_____
_____
_____
_____
_____
_____
_____
_____
_____
_____
_____
_____
_____
_____
_____
_____
_____
_____

2) Identify some situations where you were given a way out of our disease and didn't take it. How can self-awareness keep you on the right track?

_____
_____
_____
_____
_____
_____
_____
_____
_____
_____
_____
_____
_____
_____
_____
_____
_____
_____
_____
_____
_____
_____
_____
_____
_____
_____
_____
_____
_____
_____
_____

Look over your (2) journal questions and identify **_all_** your prominent issues in these situations. List them in the spaces below:

_____   _____   _____
_____   _____   _____
_____   _____   _____

Lesson:

Today, I choose to live a life of choice, not chance.

"This Time"

Full of confidence to tackle the world on my own,
But to encounter the new environment I felt very alone.

Obstacles immediately started coming my way,
Keeping insecurities inside, hoping that they would go away.

Rejection in employment began tearing down my self-esteem,
Not taking advantage of my support group,
I lost the battle to stay clean.

Still holding on to the tools once given to me,
Entering the world of drugs, while maintaining some sort of dignity.

Feeling the changes that were doing on inside,
A certain inner peace, even then I couldn't hide.

Overwhelmed with shame, feeling I didn't succeed,
Never making it this far, another chance is all I need.

Learning from my mistakes I must crawl once again,
For walking too soon, my dreams were blown away in the wind.

With God's help, a life of sobriety can truly be defined,
Through wisdom of my mistakes, determined to make it …

"This Time"
2/3/93

Written by:
Brenda Jones

FOOD FOR THOUGHT

Use your mistakes as an opportunity to get it right the next time.

Journal Questions:

1) What are some obstacles you faced where arrogance kept you stuck? How did fear of rejection play a part?

_____
_____
_____
_____
_____
_____
_____
_____
_____
_____
_____
_____
_____
_____
_____
_____
_____
_____
_____
_____
_____
_____
_____
_____
_____
_____
_____
_____
_____
_____
_____

2) When has your confidence blocked you from learning the lesson? How could you have changed the outcome?

_____

_____

_____

_____

_____

3) Identify a time when your dreams were shattered? How did moving too fast hinder your success?

_____
_____
_____
_____
_____
_____
_____
_____
_____
_____
_____
_____
_____
_____
_____
_____
_____
_____
_____
_____
_____
_____
_____
_____
_____
_____
_____
_____
_____

Look over your (3) journal questions and identify _**all**_ your prominent issues in these situations. List them in the spaces below:

_____   _____   _____
_____   _____   _____
_____   _____   _____

Lesson:

Awareness is the key to learning in all life's experiences.

"The Hood"

Life is based on what you want, not actually need,
Survival loses its meaning, becoming pure and simple greed.

Your level of intelligence is geared to the street,
Feeling a part of, you'll practice selfishness and deceit.

Respect for the game is now a thing of the past,
Getting over on anyone becomes your daily task.

Your job is to hustle – there's no room for shame,
Changing facades at will, so no one peeps your game.

Living in the fast lane is what's happening, some might say,
Falling deeper into destruction, reality slowly slips away.

The battle of survival between evil and good,
Overwhelming odds of temptation, you'll become a loser in …

"The Hood"
6/3/93

Written by:
Brenda Jones

FOOD FOR THOUGHT

Our environment nurtures our state of mind and our behaviors.

Journal Questions:

1) What are some behaviors you've displayed in the past that bring you shame today? How can you make up today by making better choices?

_____
_____
_____
_____
_____
_____
_____
_____
_____
_____
_____
_____
_____
_____
_____
_____
_____
_____
_____
_____
_____
_____
_____
_____
_____
_____
_____
_____
_____
_____
_____
_____

2) When has your wants in life kept you from appreciating what you had? How has this philosophy changed?

_____
_____
_____
_____
_____
_____
_____
_____
_____
_____
_____
_____
_____
_____
_____
_____
_____
_____
_____
_____
_____
_____
_____
_____
_____
_____
_____
_____
_____
_____
_____
_____
_____
_____
_____
_____

3) What can you do to stay focused to avoid negative temptations? How can you use past experiences to accomplish this?

_____
_____
_____
_____
_____
_____
_____
_____
_____
_____
_____
_____
_____
_____
_____
_____
_____
_____
_____
_____
_____
_____
_____
_____
_____
_____
_____
_____
_____
_____
_____

Look over your (3) journal questions and identify **_all_** your prominent issues in these situations. List them in the spaces below:

_____   _____   _____
_____   _____   _____
_____   _____   _____

Lesson:

Today, my actions will promote good character in all that I do.

"Faces"

Holding back tears to camouflage my hurt,
A mask of confidence hides my lack of self-worth.

A feeling of serenity often engulfs my heart,
Then the insecurities infiltrate my soul, tearing me apart.

The smile of a woman shielding the loneliness inside,
Overwhelmed at times, as self-defeating emotions collide.

My eyes aren't as convincing as the outer shell,
Within there is turbulence, but very few can really tell.

An existence influences by people and places,
Adapting to situations I can project many ...

"Faces"
4/11/93

Written by:
Brenda Jones

FOOD FOR THOUGHT

Embrace and grow from all that you are.

Journal Questions:

1) When has your emotional insecurities created unnecessary stress? How does this relate to past experiences?

_____

_____

_____

_____

_____

_____

_____

_____

_____

_____

_____

_____

_____

_____

_____

_____

_____

_____

_____

_____

_____

_____

_____

_____

_____

_____

_____

_____

_____

_____

_____

_____

_____

2) When has your loneliness led you in making a bad decision? How has that
   encounter affected your self-worth?

_____

_____

_____

_____

_____

_____

_____

_____

_____

_____

_____

_____

_____

_____

_____

_____

_____

_____

_____

_____

_____

_____

_____

_____

_____

_____

_____

_____

_____

_____

_____

_____

_____

3) When have you felt safe enough to confide your fears? How has your perception of "trust" changed?

_____
_____
_____
_____
_____
_____
_____
_____
_____
_____
_____
_____
_____
_____
_____
_____
_____
_____
_____
_____
_____
_____
_____
_____
_____
_____
_____
_____
_____
_____
_____

Look over your (3) journal questions and identify __*all*__ your prominent issues in these situations. List them in the spaces below:

_____   _____   _____
_____   _____   _____
_____   _____   _____

Lesson:

Today, authenticity is my guide to inner peace.

"Blessings"

Blessings come to you all the time,
Don't take them for granted when they are divinely defined.

God has always known what is best for you,
Controlling your destiny and the things you do.

He has blessed you over and over again,
Evaluate your life, before those complaints begin.

So much love is shown towards you every day,
God will provide each night as you pray.

Don't stress out on superficial things,
Enjoy what you have and count your …

"Blessings"
5/4/93

Written by:
Brenda Jones

FOOD FOR THOUGHT

To be blessed is in "knowing" that you are.

Journal Questions:

1) Identify a time when you felt there was no hope. How did you get through the hard times?

_____
_____
_____
_____
_____
_____
_____
_____
_____
_____
_____
_____
_____
_____
_____
_____
_____
_____
_____
_____
_____
_____
_____
_____
_____
_____
_____
_____
_____
_____

2) When has your self-will destroyed a blessing from God? How many times did God give you a sign you were in "His way?

_____
_____
_____
_____
_____
_____
_____
_____
_____
_____
_____
_____
_____
_____
_____
_____
_____
_____
_____
_____
_____
_____
_____
_____
_____
_____
_____
_____
_____
_____
_____
_____
_____
_____
_____

3) What superficial things clouded your view on the "real" blessing? How have you grown since then?

_____
_____
_____
_____
_____
_____
_____
_____
_____
_____
_____
_____
_____
_____
_____
_____
_____
_____
_____
_____
_____
_____
_____
_____
_____
_____
_____
_____
_____

Look over your (3) journal questions and identify **_all_** your prominent issues in these situations. List them in the spaces below:

_____   _____   _____
_____   _____   _____
_____   _____   _____

Lesson:

Today, my blessings come when I least expect them.

"I Wish"

I wish for a chance at starting over again,
Being self-sufficient with no need to pretend.

Settling for nothing but the absolute best,
Feeling secure in the abilities, I often confess.

I wish that days of clouded skies go away,
God gives me wisdom to make it, just one more day.

To become the mother I know I should,
Radiating from within, reflecting only good.

With the knowledge of life I've definitely learned,
I wish for the happiness, through experience I've earned …

"I Wish"
6/1/93

Written by:
Brenda Jones

FOOD FOR THOUGHT

Thoughts create the foundation for dreams of the future.

Journal Questions:

1) When has your self-sufficiency been a shield for your inadequacies? How did you cope with the pressure of pretending?

_____

_____

_____

_____

_____

_____

_____

_____

_____

_____

_____

_____

_____

_____

_____

_____

_____

_____

_____

_____

_____

_____

_____

_____

_____

_____

_____

_____

_____

_____

_____

_____

_____

_____

2) When has someone noticed a quality in you that lifted your self-worth? How
   have you used it to better yourself?

_____
_____
_____
_____
_____
_____
_____
_____
_____
_____
_____
_____
_____
_____
_____
_____
_____
_____
_____
_____
_____
_____
_____
_____
_____
_____
_____
_____
_____
_____
_____
_____
_____
_____
_____
_____
_____
_____

3) Identify a situation where you were given a chance to start over. What were the benefits and how did you grow spiritually?

_____
_____
_____
_____
_____
_____
_____
_____
_____
_____
_____
_____
_____
_____
_____
_____
_____
_____
_____
_____
_____
_____
_____
_____
_____
_____
_____
_____
_____

Look over your (3) journal questions and identify **_all_** your prominent issues in these situations. List them in the spaces below:

_____   _____   _____
_____   _____   _____
_____   _____   _____

Lesson:

My potential to succeed starts believing in "me".

"Shining Star"

Such innocence of the son I helped to conceive,
Making the right choices is what I believed.

As a child he was wise beyond his years,
Through my laughter, he saw the hidden tears.

Always contributing to those hard times,
Hoping his efforts would make everything fine.

Life became out of control, turning out real bad,
Destroying the bond mother and son once had.

He continued to grow, being the best he could,
Remembering only the bad times and forgetting those that were good.

Never forget "I love you", wherever you are,
Regardless of my actions, you've always been my ...

"Shining Star"
8/4/94

Written by:
Brenda Jones

FOOD FOR THOUGHT

The challenges of life doesn't diminish the love of family.

Journal Questions:

1) What choices have you made that had adversely affected your family or children?

_____
_____
_____
_____
_____
_____
_____
_____
_____
_____
_____
_____
_____
_____
_____
_____
_____
_____
_____
_____
_____
_____
_____
_____
_____
_____
_____
_____

2) When has your family or children been your inspiration to do better? How can you be an inspiration to them today?

_____

_____

_____

_____

_____

_____

_____

_____

_____

_____

_____

_____

_____

_____

_____

_____

_____

_____

_____

_____

_____

_____

_____

_____

_____

_____

_____

_____

_____

_____

_____

_____

_____

_____

_____

_____

_____

3) In what ways has your past experiences strengthened your bond? How do you show love for them now?

_____
_____
_____
_____
_____
_____
_____
_____
_____
_____
_____
_____
_____
_____
_____
_____
_____
_____
_____
_____
_____
_____
_____
_____
_____
_____
_____

Look over your (3) journal questions and identify **_all_** your prominent issues in these situations. List them in the spaces below:

_____   _____   _____
_____   _____   _____
_____   _____   _____

Lesson:

Today, I will inspire my loved ones by example.

"Through It All"

Strangers meeting for the very first time,
Our bond grew stronger, as real friendship was defined.

Sharing a past life of great emotional pain,
We realized even though different, we're the same.

We laughed a lot and often cried,
But no matter what, we stood by each others' side

An unspoken trust without words being said,
Now growing in a positive way, from our lifestyles we led.

A closeness so sincere, it can't be torn apart,
Even when far away, you're close to my heart.

A silent strength if either should fall,
Our friendship will continue to endure …

"Through It All"
1/7/94

Written by:
Brenda Jones

FOOD FOR THOUGHT

A strong friendship endures the test of time.

Journal Questions:

1) When have you connected with someone immediately, feeling it was destiny? How did that relationship grow?

_____

_____

_____

_____

_____

_____

_____

_____

_____

_____

_____

_____

_____

_____

_____

_____

_____

_____

_____

_____

_____

_____

_____

_____

_____

_____

_____

_____

_____

2) Identify a situation where a friendship was threatened? How did "trust" play a part in strengthening the bond?

_____
_____
_____
_____
_____
_____
_____
_____
_____
_____
_____
_____
_____
_____
_____
_____
_____
_____
_____
_____
_____
_____
_____
_____
_____
_____
_____
_____
_____
_____
_____
_____
_____
_____
_____
_____
_____
_____
_____

3) When did sharing an emotional pain bring you closer to a friend? How did that experience enrich your life?

_____
_____
_____
_____
_____
_____
_____
_____
_____
_____
_____
_____
_____
_____
_____
_____
_____
_____
_____
_____
_____
_____
_____
_____
_____
_____
_____
_____

Look over your (3) journal questions and identify **_all_** your prominent issues in these situations. List them in the spaces below:

_____   _____   _____
_____   _____   _____
_____   _____   _____

Lesson:

My friendship will never let you down.

"My Child"

Remembering his birth, I beamed with great pride that beautiful son,
Which I carried inside.

I begin my journey to be the best mother,
A team, I loved him like no other.

So innocent and pure, it was apparent in his eyes,
The intelligence he possessed even then wasn't any surprise.

Life started to be really good,
I took responsibility that every mother should.

Then drugs entered my life, destroying what we had,
Regrets of that time, makes me so sad.

My life became unmanageable and I sent him away,
A decision that haunts me each and every day.

I've lost his love because of chemical abuse,
He thinks as a mother, for him, I have no use.

I made promises to turn my life around,
But through my addiction, I continually let him down.

Now, I must show him that I can go that extra mile,
To regain the trust and love of ...

"My Child"
1/25/94

Written by:
Brenda Jones

FOOD FOR THOUGHT

Honor those you love by making a change.

Journal Questions:

1) What were your goals for being a good parent? How did you allow outside forces to distract you?

_____

_____

_____

_____

_____

_____

_____

_____

_____

_____

_____

_____

_____

_____

_____

_____

_____

_____

_____

_____

_____

_____

_____

_____

_____

_____

_____

_____

_____

_____

_____

2) What regretful decisions have you made, causing harm to those you love? How have those choices affected your relationships?

_____
_____
_____
_____
_____
_____
_____
_____
_____
_____
_____
_____
_____
_____
_____
_____
_____
_____
_____
_____
_____
_____
_____
_____
_____
_____
_____
_____
_____
_____
_____
_____
_____
_____
_____
_____
_____
_____
_____

3) When did idle promises destroy your family's trust? How can you regain their trust by going the extra mile?

_____
_____
_____
_____
_____
_____
_____
_____
_____
_____
_____
_____
_____
_____
_____
_____
_____
_____
_____
_____
_____
_____
_____
_____
_____
_____
_____
_____
_____
_____

Look over your (3) journal questions and identify _**all**_ your prominent issues in these situations. List them in the spaces below:

_____   _____   _____
_____   _____   _____
_____   _____   _____

Lesson:

My quest for acceptance starts with my commitment to change.

-59-

"Tell Someone"

Tormented visions of unwarranted shame,
Out of my control, I took the blame.

My innocence violated in the worst conceivable way,
Consumed with guilt, it seems both night and day.

Feeling less than, the dark secrets I'd keep,
An experience of betrayal I would inwardly weep.

A voice of hope somehow surfaces within,
I wasn't alone, somewhere there's a real friend.

So, reach out and express those images of despair,
You'll be surprised at how many people care.

A villain runs free because of what they've done,
You're not at fault, please …

"Tell Someone"
3/11/94

Written by:
Brenda Jones

FOOD FOR THOUGHT

Share a secret and heal your soul.

Journal Questions:

1) When have you kept a childhood secret because you felt ashamed? How did you cope with the betrayal?

_____

_____

_____

_____

_____

_____

_____

_____

_____

_____

_____

_____

_____

_____

_____

_____

_____

_____

_____

_____

_____

_____

_____

_____

_____

_____

_____

_____

_____

_____

_____

2) How did your life change after the event? How did that experience affect your relationships with others?

_____
_____
_____
_____
_____
_____
_____
_____
_____
_____
_____
_____
_____
_____
_____
_____
_____
_____
_____
_____
_____
_____
_____
_____
_____
_____
_____
_____
_____
_____
_____
_____
_____
_____
_____
_____
_____
_____

3) When did you regain your dignity back and how did sharing the secret empower you?

_____
_____
_____
_____
_____
_____
_____
_____
_____
_____
_____
_____
_____
_____
_____
_____
_____
_____
_____
_____
_____
_____
_____
_____
_____
_____
_____
_____
_____
_____
_____

Look over your (3) journal questions and identify **_all_** your prominent issues in these situations. List them in the spaces below:

_____   _____   _____
_____   _____   _____
_____   _____   _____

Lesson:

The truth will break the chains that bind me.

-63-

"Give Him Praise"

He watches over us during the many times of despair,
Through His Holy Spirit, for us, He's always there.

Dealing with life's pitfalls, He'll help us to be strong,
Loving us unconditionally, no matter if we're right or wrong.

He patiently waits while we often go astray,
That divine and silent protection never goes away.

Our faith is tested regarding life and its simple greed,
Realizing salvation is the only way to accomplish satisfaction guaranteed.

Sacrificing His life so we would have better days,
Walk in His light, not our own and ...

"Give Him Praise"
1/15/94

Written by:
Brenda Jones

FOOD FOR THOUGHT

Trust in a power you cannot see.

Journal Questions:

1) Identify a situation where you felt a "power" protecting you. How did you explain the outcome?

_____

_____

_____

_____

_____

_____

_____

_____

_____

_____

_____

_____

_____

_____

_____

_____

_____

_____

_____

_____

_____

_____

_____

_____

_____

_____

_____

_____

_____

_____

_____

2) When have you taken credit for God's work? How did that decision cloud your judgment?

_____
_____
_____
_____
_____
_____
_____
_____
_____
_____
_____
_____
_____
_____
_____
_____
_____
_____
_____
_____
_____
_____
_____
_____
_____
_____
_____
_____
_____
_____
_____
_____
_____
_____

3) When was your faith tested? How could surrendering make things easier?

_____
_____
_____
_____
_____
_____
_____
_____
_____
_____
_____
_____
_____
_____
_____
_____
_____
_____
_____
_____
_____
_____
_____
_____
_____
_____
_____
_____
_____
_____
_____
_____

Look over your (3) journal questions and identify **_all_** your prominent issues in these situations. List them in the spaces below:

_____   _____   _____
_____   _____   _____
_____   _____   _____

Lesson:

I have no power without God's power.

"Out of Darkness"

Feelings are no longer guarded behind a closed door,
A life with no direction, I want no more.

Simple things excite me, like the beauty of nature's trees,
Realizing that myself, I must first try to please.

Constantly growing as I reflect on where I've been,
Discarding a lifestyle which I must always defend.

Knowing I'm meant to live much better than this,
As I attempt my journey ...

"Out of Darkness"
3/6/93

Written by:
Brenda Jones

FOOD FOR THOUGHT

You will go without, if you can't speak from within.

Journal Questions:

1) When has sharing a secret produced negative results? How did that one experience create a wall of defense?

_____

_____

_____

_____

_____

_____

_____

_____

_____

_____

_____

_____

_____

_____

_____

_____

_____

_____

_____

_____

_____

_____

_____

_____

_____

_____

_____

_____

_____

_____

_____

_____

2) What was your turning point in becoming vulnerable? How has that moment enhanced your life?

_____

_____

_____

_____

_____

_____

_____

_____

_____

_____

_____

_____

_____

_____

_____

_____

_____

_____

_____

_____

_____

_____

_____

_____

_____

_____

_____

_____

_____

_____

_____

_____

_____

_____

_____

3) How has holding onto your past been a liability? How important is remembering where you came from? Why?

_____
_____
_____
_____
_____
_____
_____
_____
_____
_____
_____
_____
_____
_____
_____
_____
_____
_____
_____
_____
_____
_____
_____
_____
_____
_____
_____
_____
_____
_____

Look over your (3) journal questions and identify **_all_** your prominent issues in these situations. List them in the spaces below:

_____   _____   _____
_____   _____   _____
_____   _____   _____

Lesson:

The sunlight shines through my willingness to be honest.

-71-

"Someday"

People won't be judged because of the color of their skin,
The young won't die for the turn they defend.

Nuclear war will be a thing of the past,
The hungry won't think of this meal as their last.

Drugs won't be a way to run from pain,
Now will there be hospitals for the mentally insane.

Love will be a commitment, not just a word,
While testimonies from God will not longer go unheard.

Children will have respect for themselves as well as others,
Being positive role models as fathers and mothers.

Without working together, these things won't go away,
Going back to basics, it will happen …

"Someday"
3/14/94

Written by:
Brenda Jones

FOOD FOR THOUGHT

I make my own reality.

Journal Questions:

1) When have you resisted positive change? How could it have benefitted you today?

_____
_____
_____
_____
_____
_____
_____
_____
_____
_____
_____
_____
_____
_____
_____
_____
_____
_____
_____
_____
_____
_____
_____
_____
_____
_____
_____
_____
_____
_____
_____
_____
_____

2) What simple ways can you start a positive change? How will you be an example to others?

_____
_____
_____
_____
_____
_____
_____
_____
_____
_____
_____
_____
_____
_____
_____
_____
_____
_____
_____
_____
_____
_____
_____
_____
_____
_____
_____
_____
_____
_____
_____
_____
_____

3) How could you make a difference in the world? What cause would you choose
and why?

_____
_____
_____
_____
_____
_____
_____
_____
_____
_____
_____
_____
_____
_____
_____
_____
_____
_____
_____
_____
_____
_____
_____
_____
_____
_____
_____
_____
_____

Look over your (3) journal questions and identify **_all_** your prominent issues in
these situations. List them in the spaces below:

_____   _____   _____
_____   _____   _____
_____   _____   _____

Lesson:

Today, I will do my part to make a difference.

Review all the journal questions. Process and notice the issues that are repeated in your journaling. In the space below, identify those that surfaced most often.

_____

_____

_____

_____

_____

My Final Thought

I've discovered over the years that perceptions change depending on that's going on in your life, as well as the environment you're in. The advantage to this philosophy and its relevance to this section are: whatever you've written down in the journal questions today will initiate a much different response in six months or one year from now. You will have the opportunity to expand your horizons and be in a constant state of evolution, while growing in self-awareness and emotional empowerment.

I have truly enjoyed sharing my intimate thoughts with you. I feel we are kindred spirits, who have finally reconnected emotionally. Because of your heartfelt commitment to process the journal questions, you have probably uncovered, discarded and discovered important information and beliefs that will enrich your perception of self. I encourage you to continue your quest of enlightenment. You must believe you deserve the best ... one day at a time.

Remember, when in doubt of who you are becoming or where you're going, find a safe place, grab a pen and embrace the journey ... "inside you".

Part II

THE SOLUTION

(Uncovering the Truth)

Table of Contents

Part II   **The Solution (Uncovering the Truth)**

Page

INTRODUCTION

"Uncovering the Truth"

This is the *most* important part of your healing process. The concept for this section was definitely divinely orchestrated. Its' conception began in 2000 at the California Rehabilitation Center (CRC) in Norco. I was beginning another phase of my recovery and my life as a Substance Abuse Counselor. One of my tasks as a counselor was to facilitate all day workshops for the clients. I had some material already on relationships, so I decided that would be the subject to present. The workshop was a big hit and my supervisor suggested I teach a class on a weekly basis. Thus, began my journey to the material in this section. Two months into the class, God gave me a vision, which started with a mental picture of the Core Issue Chart (or 'firecracker', as the clients call it). I needed something simple, but powerful to achieve healing. Next, I needed an example of issues to show clients how to process the chart. As you know by the section "Inside Me", I suffered from low self-esteem and low self-worth. With 8 years in recovery, God knew I was in a place in my life where the 12 steps, AA meetings and just staying clean weren't enough. There was still a void in becoming 'whole'. I kept it simple and used myself, my pain and my childhood as the example. As I filled each circle and square, my healing into wholeness took off. I finally received peace and understanding concerning all those issues that influenced my choices of addiction, prison, unhealthy relationships and low self-esteem. I achieved the clarity to hear God when He spoke to me and He's been talking to me ever since. I have had the privilege of sharing the 'gift' of self-empowerment with over 300 women who thought like I thought and felt like I felt. On the following page are just a few of the 'revelational testimonies' detailing their journey. May their stories encourage you to embrace your own personal journey into "Uncovering the Truth".

2008 Revelations

"When it was my time to go into Family Dynamics, it wasn't soon enough! You see, I am intelligent to a fault. I drove just about everyone nuts because I knew it ALL. I could tell you anything you wanted or didn't want to know. I knew every staff member's schedule, where every resident lived, who was whose roommate, and so on."

"So entering Family Dynamics was a turning point. I found that because of all the abandonment that I suffered made me feel like I needed to know more, be smarter and maybe people would stop leaving me. I also found out that the reason I turned to drugs was because I wanted to numb the pain I felt from being abandoned. I didn't want to feel. Period. Doing the Damaged Emotions Chart was eye-opening. It gave me clarity. Doing the "firecracker" took the power out of all the crap I had survived. When I finished the Relationship Chart, it showed me why I picked such crappy mates".

Today, I feel more complete. I have a better relationship with God. He still has jokes, but I am able to laugh at them better! I have a better relationship with my son and the rest of my family."

"Having all the pieces to the puzzle makes all the difference in my life today".   M.C.   2008

"I have been al alcoholic and an addict since I was in my early teens. I was born into a family that wanted the perfect family – a girl and a boy. When I was born, I was supposed to be a boy, because they already had my sister. My brother, their *wanted* son, was born 15 months after me. So, I am a middle child and carry all the baggage that "classification" brings with it. I was always very competitive, seeking attention and affection and I carried into adulthood a need to people please. My competitive nature craved attention".

"I started this class called "Family Dynamics" and 'wasn't no one gonna teach me anything I hadn't already *accepted* and *reflected* on.' But slowly, my walls came down and my ears opened and my mouth shut. I had issues! Really!! It opened my eyes and my soul to a whole new world. I finally woke up and discovered me in the process. I let go of resentments and bitterness, discovering the woman I am now. I am empowered with knowledge and self-love and God's will …"

"Everyone has a chart and since I've done my own (Firecracker), I have a new insight into people … patience and a calm I've never known before. Family Dynamics showed me I need to love me and that I do need people in my life – my fiancé, friends, family and acquaintances. It showed me how to let go and love myself."   Audra K.   2008

"In the beginning of my journey to healing, I was a broken, 20 year old "child", seeking and craving love. I walked around with nothing but a blank look on my face, but inside, a whirlwind of confusion and hurt. Coming from a childhood of physical abuse and chaos created a lot of pain."

"The Damaged Emotions Chart gave me a chance to look back at the different times in my life that I was betrayed and hurt, but most of all, it gave me clarity on why I acted out the way I did and what situations caused it. Nobody had the answers. But then, I finally realized the answer was inside of me."

"Doing the chart, I identified all my feelings, where they came from and what my core issues were. It hit me … I looked at the chart and realized that I not only went through it, I survived it!"

"I feel I've reached healing and understanding. I'm no longer the "Lost Child", but I feel that I'm confident and don't need validation to fill that void."   Corey V.   2008

"As I began this journey, I was a smart and funny woman. One who had no problems or issues. I was not here to get help because there was 'nothing wrong with me' that needed fixing, or so I thought!"

"The broken and lost woman that I was began healing because of Family Dynamics" or "Family D", as I came to know it. Not wanting to face the realities of my childhood, I had "forgotten" the past. It didn't have anything to do with my present or my future."

"Getting to my core issue of physical abandonment was difficult to accept. Once I realized that this was the beginning of the rest of my problems … low self-esteem, co-dependency, etc. There was no going back. I went into depth with myself and could finally see what needed to be fixed – EVERYTHING! I go to the root of my problem, and today I can face my past. I am making a change in my present and with thanks to my Higher Power – my determination and "Family D", my future is going to be great!
                                                                        Kim L.   2008

Revelations (continued)

"When I started this journey of recovery, I had no idea of the things I'd learn of 'self'. I knew I wanted something different, but didn't know how to get there. I thought I could get by just doing a little work, as I thought I had it more together than others. I thought I was different."

"I was broken, confused and afraid to let anyone know me. Didn't think I had anything good to say, as my thinking was so toxic. I also thought if I looked and acted right on the outside, then everyone would believe it. When I did my Damaged Emotions Chart, it helped me to see how the things that were said and done to me weren't my fault."

"I believed that I was stupid and had to try harder to be smart. I was unsure of my thoughts. By being beat and molested, my sense of self-worth was zero, so I shut down. From this class, I now know my behavior and where it comes from and now I know how to identify it and change it. I now have my power back as a mother, daughter and woman. I no longer have to be a doormat or condemn myself. By writing my little girl, I was able to get in touch with my feelings as a child and to help the little girl that was me. Just doing that opens up a lot and heals your spirit. I look at life with new eyes."

"I became a heroin addict at 13 … I'm now 39. I no longer have to exist in darkness. I can live in the light and love myself."

Julie H. (Jewels) 2008

"I'm 36, I have 3 kids and I've been on drugs for 15 years. I was so nervous when I started this class. I did not want to bring up my past because it was too much hurt and pain behind my past. I've never dealt with this pain, because I was always hiding behind alcohol and drugs."

"But when I came to this class, I was hurt, lost and broken. When I did my Damaged Emotions Chart, it really helped me to uncover some of my pain. It opened my eyes to see that things I went through weren't my fault. Before this class, I didn't know how to love or even have any good relationships (all unhealthy) and I had bad, distorted thinking, so I never thought I was worthy. Since I've been through this class, I have found myself. I am no longer lost. I have faith. I am much stronger."

"Family Dynamics also helped me to get in touch with the inner little girl. Something I've never thought about doing. But I am standing tall through it all. I am a stronger, confident woman. I can do whatever I put my mind to. I am making better choices today."

Evette J. 2008

"When I started "Family D", I was very angry. The hurt I carried inside was heavy on my attitude. I didn't let anyone pass the wall."

"The truth of the matter was, I really hated myself for all the past regrets and I didn't have the answers. 'Family D' showed me hard core stuff – I was a much mangled, heart-resentful, broken woman inside. I knew than I blocked all my feelings. It made me cry, gave me angry and happy emotions – all emotions inside came out, issues – core issues. I really understood them now. I know that my wounds can be healed. I can have compassion toward others that do me wrong. My little girl, "Coconut" was deprived and neglected. Her fears and insecurities … her desperate need to be loved lives inside me and I will take the time to love and care for her. I know now I don't and will not use to numb me. I have knowledge now that's to live within me. I will fight to be who I need to be to live … because I no longer have to die."

Coco 2008

"I'm a 40 year old woman. I have two sons – ages 20 and 17. I've been doing drugs for half my life. I've been in and out of jail and prison for the last 10 years. When I finally got here, I was so broken and closed up; I was full of so much hurt and resentments."

"The first day of 'Family D' was very emotional for me. One reason was because I got to hear stories of other women and they almost sounded like mine. I was molested by my stepfather. This event in my life has left me a very damaged woman. I have resentments that have been holding me down and filling me with hate and anger for over 30 years. Now that I know my core issue, I understand why I used drugs for so long. I've always thought I did dope because I liked it. I never knew I was doing it to numb all of my hurts and pains from my childhood. Thanks to 'Family D', I feel I have a second chance for a better life. I know I'm worth it! I feel like a gigantic weight has been lifted."

Traci P. 2008

Final Destination ... Alumni Revelations – Men

"I grew up in a violent household, in a violent neighborhood and joined a violent gang. I didn't know for years that I was on a road less traveled. At 56 years ole, I found myself still using, still on parole and without any clear picture of myself. I knew it wasn't my past, but today's man seemed haunted and vacant. I was a man going through the motions, no personal connections and no skills to get anywhere. The sad part of this is it all felt normal to me. I entered Family Dynamics and the first thing that struck me was how Brenda brought (7) hard core convicts, wet in their ways of not trusting and not feeling, together (the very things that had eluded us for years). She replaced them with trust and a common goal of self-realization. Three weeks later I was brought through a fire that had burned me for over forth years. The release and freedom is hard to describe other than to say I came to the Lighthouse thinking I was a lost cause. Today I KNOW I am the matter that matters and can rebuild my life into a success story!"   Steven Z. (forever grateful) 2009

"I entered Brenda's Family Dynamics class with reservations. I did not believe it had anything to offer me. As far as I was concerned, my childhood was at worse, an average happy one. I still try to hold on to that delusion at times. After completing the first day of this course ... I was an emotional wreck! It seems I had many childhood issues that I had left suppressed and unresolved. Brenda's guidance helped me to piece scattered knowledge into a very clear picture of the core issues that led me to a life of violence and drug addiction. I will be forever grateful for the lessons learned in the Family Dynamics class. Brenda's approach made me discover a clear view of my past in a very short period of time. I believe some people may go through years of other therapy at great expense and never will they achieve the clarity I have now. Thank you, Brenda, ever so much!
                                 David S.   2009

"Growing up in Long Beach, CA was an experience worth talking about. At an early age, my family and I lived in the projects of the city. My relationship with my parents, and later my little sister, was a normal one, or so I thought. The "Family Dynamics" class brought to light some very interesting points that I had stuffed in the back of my mind for years unaware of the destruction they caused in my adult life. The memories were so suppressed that I justified the pain, which escalated my decent to hard drugs and the lifestyle that went with the pain. The class helped me to uncover the root of my pain. My life, at 62 years old, is by NO means over! Today, I feel I have a purpose in life and truly feel closer to my Higher Power and one day at a time can accomplish that purpose!
                                 Alvin K.   2009

"When I first started 'Family D", I didn't know what to expect and frankly, I was scared of what I would discover. As the class went on and I found out things that happened to me as a child, I realized those things played a huge part in all y adult decisions and behaviors. At a young age, I started drinking and doing drugs, eventually landing in prison. After a decade in prison I felt lost. This class has opened my eyes and today I have a sense off clarity. Not only am I dealing with my addiction, but I have a better understanding of myself. Brenda Jones helped me realize who I really am and helped me to break free of the baggage I've been carrying around for years. I highly recommend this class to anyone who wants to discover who they are. My life ahead is much brighter, filled with hope and a future of success.   Frank B.
2009

"My name is Edward Corona. I am 46 years old and have spent nearly 30 years battling drug addiction, incarceration, not including the seven years in juvenile facilities. Spending most of my life behind walls, I felt safe and secure. I have nothing to worry about. As a child, I grew up with no real direction or attention given to me. My parents gave me material things like toys to show me love. What I didn't get, I threw tantrums and eventually got whatever it was I wanted. My childhood was a blur. It was someone else ... not me. My parents, being alcoholics and much older (my father is 66 and my mom is 45) didn't help. I was also the last child born, so I was really left to my own devices. At 12, I started to experiment with drugs and alcohol, later becoming a heroin addict at 20. To this day, I regret what I've done, but on the same note, I'm free from my past, a past that held me captive to its' alluring delusions of fun, fame and fortune. A dream disabled by heroin and prison. I was completely consumed with these two activities that nothing was sacred. I crossed many boundaries, hurt many people, throwing my life into a grave, a prison yard and heroin. After 12 years of seeking recovery, my trial brought me to the 'Family D' class. I found the lost little boy who never had a chance to grow up properly. I know what part I played and found out who I really am. Today, I know who I am ... A man on a mission in the field of recovery.
                                 Edward C.   2009

"From death to life. After years of humiliation, degradation and incarceration ... today I'm in a place of refuge and safety. I know it is possible for me to live free of the shackles of my past. You see, I am a hope to die dope fiend who had accepted the reality that I would die in the streets from an overdose, gun shot, knife or spend 25-to-live in a jail cell as a 3rd striker.

"My condition seemed hopeless. My dignity, self-respect, hope and dreams all died almost from the gate. I lost my wife, kids, cars and my home. I lost my identity and my soul. In my early years, I burned everyone out, both family and friends. My health followed shortly after. I lost my teeth, contracted Hep C, was shot, stabbed, jumped, shanked, beat with sticks, poisoned and eventually hit by a car (almost losing my ability to walk). Scariest of all, I then caught a case of cocaine and faced my worst nightmare ... 25 to life! By the grace of God, I was given 3 ½ years in state prison. After serving 19 months, I returned to the streets where I tried hard as hell to kill myself. I didn't want to be there, doing the same things that had cost me so much, but I was powerless! I had been on ice for 19 months. My addiction was alive and kicking as strong as ever. After being away for 19 months, I lasted 9 days before being violated and returned to state prison again."

"This was perhaps the biggest blessing of my life. After 8 months, I was sent to a residential program for parolees. The clinical coordinator, Brenda Jones, encouraged us all to take her Family Dynamics class which she had taught the women for years. The class was now being offered to the men since she was the clinical coordinator. At first, I was very resistant to the idea that my life of destructive behaviors had anything to do with my childhood. We didn't have a Cosby-like family, but there was not a lot of outward dysfunction either. After a period of reflection and introspection, I realized this was far from the truth. The family dynamics class helped me to shine a bright light into closets I had closed off years ago. Through the therapeutic process and the guidance of Brenda Jones, I've cleaned out these closets and, today, I understand why my life has been so full of turmoil. Brenda helped me to escape the skeletons that had me a prisoner for so long. Today, I feel a sense of freedom I never knew existed. I had all this stuff just bottled inside. I finally exited and have taken a drink from the spring of hope and happiness. I have a profound sense of gratitude and recommend the "Family Dynamics" class to anyone searching for the reason why. Free yourself and breathe. Here's a shout out to Brenda for leading me to the light of my soul. For the addict out there suffering ... just know that you are not at fault for your past, but you are responsible for your future. Reach out a hand and take hold of living in the life!

Keith H. PEACE! 2009

Professional Observations

"I have had the opportunity to witness the life-changing experiences of women that have taken the "Family Dynamics" class at the Department of Corrections at CRC ('New Starts'), from 2000-2—5. The women arrived very broken with low self-esteem and were unable to connect with anyone, including themselves. They were resistant to change, and in most instances, full of denial and defiance."

"Once these women were introduced to 'Family Dynamics', they began to gain and understand what relationships were and how it related to their choices, as adults. They realized that building healthy relationships and changing behaviors took time; regaining self-esteem is a process and requires a lot of emotional work. It also gave them an insight into coming to terms with their core issues. These women's transformation shocked not only the person involved, but others in the community. The dictionary defines *metamorphosis as 1) A change of physical form, structure or substance, 2) As a striking alteration (as in appearance or character)*. This indeed is what 'Family Dynamics' class has accomplished for many women. They finally embraced and reaped all the benefits of healing from the class. The most important part of 'Family Dynamics' class starts with learning to love themselves first."

Mildred Jenkins, RDA, FACT, BA
Supervising Counselor
Dept. of Corrections and Rehabilitation
Calif. Institute for Women ('New Starts')

"Dear Reader: I am writing this testimonial to emphasize the importance and value of the lessons presented in this workbook. As an individual who has been exposed to and touched by the heart-breaking disease of addiction, I found myself looking for the causes of such painful and self-destructive behavior. As a Medical Research Scientist, I had found that medicine was not able to give me the answers I needed to completely explain the causes of addiction, so I sought out answers at the psychological level. Through praises from her former clients, I decided to meet with Brenda and ask her to observe and eventually participate in her 'Family Dynamics' class. Women case to this class as a part of the rehabilitation process from their addiction and learned the answers to their biggest question: 'Why have I done what I have done?' Through a process of self-discovery, women learn the reasons why they started to abuse drugs/alcohol and learn to forgive those people in their life that caused their pain. But, more importantly, they learn why they continue certain behavior and make the choices they do, as adults. Sitting in her class, and participating in the work, I was able to see how the way in which I was raised has contributed to my positive attributes of motivation, which have led to my academic and professional achievements. I was also able to become aware of my role in the problems I have encountered in my interpersonal relationships and the reasons for which I sabotage them. The greatest benefit of this class is that it brings enlightenment to those who participate. It changes women from the "victim" role to blaming their parents, to giving them the power to change through understanding and forgiveness. Armed with that knowledge, these women now have that option to change their lives and leave the circle of emotional and addictive self-destructive behavior. I would recommend this work to anyone who finds themselves wondering the answer to that difficult question – 'How does this keep happening to me?' Because the answers, and change, lie within. Thank you, Brenda."

Sangita N. Shah, Ph.D.

"Readers: I had the opportunity to work with Brenda Jones as the Program Director for the New Starts Therapeutic Community at the California Rehabilitation Center for over five years."

"Brenda had the ability to draw from her own experiences and the stories of countless women who entered the program and ultimately began their own personal journey at that magical time. The 'Relationship' class she taught was a class that women first feared and then sought when they knew that there were core issues that had to be addressed. The women who completed this class were always very proud of the process they had gone through and always recommended it to the ones behind them when the time was right. I admire the way Brenda sought to build on the tools she had personally, and was always "revamping" her work to fit the needs of the women in the process. She developed a curriculum that she is proud of and she knows it has helped the women in their sobriety and I recommend that all women, either new or seeking to discover more about themselves, engage in this process with the tools she has developed."

"We know that there is always more to reveal, more to learn and ways that we can grow in developing our sense of self. Brenda has done a wonderful job at becoming a 'phenomenal woman'."

Sincerely, Deanna Moody-Kivett, CATC, FACT
Mental Health Systems – Program Manager

Destination ... Family Dysfunction

Our issues originate from the family of origin, which is a vital part of our development as adults. There are many components influencing that phase of our development. It is important to fully understand all four components in order to achieve a clear canvas of who you are and why. Family dysfunction, witnessed by a child, evolves into family dysfunction as an adult.

Four Components of Family Dysfunction:

1) **Overt Mental Abuse:** Your primary caretaker uses you as a scapegoat to vent their own personal frustrations or inadequacies, which surfaces through different forms of physical, verbal or sexual abuse. This can cause a lifetime of self-destructive behavior to the person subjected to this type of abuse.

2) **Intrinsic Abuse:** Primary caretaker stifles your development by not supplying the emotional nurturing required for successful transition into adulthood. Acts of praise, encouragement and positive memories that often reinforce a child's self-confidence is lacking. Caretaker is either too focused on self or simply unable to show any nurturing qualities.

3) **Emotionally Absent:** Caretaker unavailable because of pre-occupation with other priorities they feel are more important such as relationships, work and drugs/alcohol. Any of these distractions by caretaker diverts necessary attention from you, causing you to take the role of parenting yourself.

4) **Denial:** Emotional needs as a child aren't met because caretaker is suffering from inability to address the problems in the family and they act out in inappropriate ways in order to cope with these shortcomings. You are left lost and confused with no adult supervision or direction.

Identify at least two of the four Family Dysfunctions you can relate to. This will be an essential part of processing your Core Chart later on.

Family Dysfunction:

_____
_____
_____
_____
_____
_____
_____
_____

How did you cope with this in your life?

_____
_____
_____
_____
_____
_____
_____
_____

Family Dysfunction:

_____
_____
_____
_____
_____
_____
_____

How did you cope with this in your life?

_____
_____
_____
_____
_____
_____
_____
_____

Destination … Damaged Emotion Chart

To acquire the solution, we must start at the inner core of our belief system and the events that set the stage or, if you will, lay the foundation for our adult development. The experience of embracing the truth requires ***total honesty***, a lot of painful memories, and a complete commitment to walk through that pain. We adapt to powerful coping skills or defense mechanisms (usually subconsciously and destructive) in order to cope and erase the pain. This results in many self-destructive behaviors, i.e., low self-esteem, co-dependency, unhealthy relationships, addiction, alcoholism, etc. To address any of those destructive behaviors requires examining the early childhood pain outlined in the damaged emotion chart.

Directions for Processing Chart:

HURT: Use ages 0 – 13 as a reference point of identifying your earliest childhood hurt or trauma. These are usually the ages emotional development occurs and is most damaging to adults. The damage is already done by the teen years.

BELIEF: Based on the hurt, we often create a belief system in order to cope with the messages sent. We act out in inappropriate ways to life's events.

GOAL: Because you believe messages acquired in early childhood, you subconsciously adapt self-defeating behaviors reinforcing your belief.

BEHAVIOR (Child):
Actions acquired as a child that reinforced your belief caused by the hurt.

BEHAVIOR (Adult):
Actions of self-destruction carried into adulthood from your childhood.

UNCOVERED EMOTIONS:
What are the emotions manifested from your childhood hurt, i.e., Anger, Unworthy, Isolation, Fear, etc.

DAMAGED EMOTIONS

HURT (Include ages)	DISCOVER BELIEF (instilled by hurt)	GOAL (based on belief)	DISCARD (Behavior as a child)	DISCARD (Behavior transformed into adulthood)	UNCOVERED EMOTIONS (created by hurt)

CHILDHOOD NEGATIVE MESSAGES

REVIEW QUESTIONS

These are some questions that should be answered in two (2) parts. First, look at them from the Damaged Emotion Chart of your childhood hut or trauma. Then, answer them as an adult living through those experiences. This will allow you to examine your unconscious loyalties you may have to inaccurate information.

Childhood:
1) What did I believe about myself?

_____
_____
_____

2) How did I demonstrate this belief?

_____
_____
_____

3) What did I remember being told about myself?

_____
_____
_____

4) How did my behavior support what I've been told?

_____
_____
_____

Adulthood:
1) What do I believe about myself?

_____
_____
_____

2) How do I demonstrate this belief?

_____
_____
_____

3) What do I remember being told about myself?

_____
_____
_____

4) How does my behavior support what I've been told?

_____
_____
_____

Summary – Damaged Emotions Chart

Here's your opportunity to express the clarity you've obtained from the Damaged Emotions Chart. Be *detailed* in addressing the Hurt, Belief, Goal, Behavior and Emotion, based on your chart. You'll be amazed at the freedom that self-awareness gives you.

_____
_____
_____
_____
_____
_____
_____
_____
_____
_____
_____
_____
_____
_____
_____
_____
_____
_____
_____
_____
_____
_____
_____
_____
_____
_____
_____
_____
_____
_____
_____
_____
_____
_____
_____

Destination ... Healing into Wholeness
(Your Inner Child)

Working through the previous segment, you are probably overwhelmed with what you've uncovered and are feeling a little exposed, vulnerable and uncomfortable. That's your inner child whose pain has been unleashed. To achieve effective adult growth, it is essential to nurture your inner child through their early experiences of trauma and pain. Over the years, you've attempted to cover up these events with relationships, addictions, material possessions and the void created in early childhood festers like an unhealed sore, spilling over into everything you touch. It's time to nurture your inner child with the love, support and compassion that only _you_ can give.

DIRECTIONS: **Journaling Your Inner Child**

- **<u>FIRST ENTRY</u>:** Introduce yourself to them. Bring them up on what you've been doing and let them know that you've realized through life and recovery that you forgot them. Make a commitment to write them and keep your commitment.

- **ALL OTHER ENTRIES FOLLOW THESE STEPS BELOW:**

1) Write to them to connect to their hurt and yours. The process will not work otherwise. <u>YOU</u> will remain the victim, taking the focus off of _them_

2) Always start your entry with an update of your day, thoughts or progress ... THEN –

3) Nurture them through (1) of the hurts you've outlined on your Damaged Emotions Chart. Only a _brief_ description of the hurt is necessary, otherwise again, <u>YOU</u> take the victim role.

4) Tell _them_ what _they_ needed to hear during that hurtful situation for comfort. USE A LOT OF SPACE HERE. <u>THIS IS THE MOST IMPORTANT PART</u>!

5) <u>ALWAYS</u> take _them_ to do something fun before ending your session. You don't want to leave _yourself_ or _them_ open and sad, but at peace and free!

6) If you had a nickname as a child, _use_ it when nurturing your inner child. This enables you to identify that period in your life more accurately.

7) Having a picture of yourself as a child is also very helpful. "Look at your eyes in that picture ... they are the windows to your soul.

Examples of How to Journal Your Inner Child

Dear Louie:

Hi, it's me – Linda   ☺

It's been a long time since I've acknowledged you. I always knew you were here inside me. I just plainly ignored you. I thought if I tucked you away, all my pain would go away. Difference was, the pain belonged to both of us and I never gave you a chance to get ride of your pain. The good thing is I'm ready to help you. I'm ready to try and recognize our pain together. Now, when I look back at all the time I felt this void in my heart and know more than ever now that that void was your place. I left an empty spot for you and today you're going to fill that spot. Welcome home, little one. I've missed you terribly and though I've felt you inside me, today I'm including you in every day of my life. You'll never have to be alone and you'll never have to feel abandoned. I love you very much and I remember everything you've gone through. From that time when you were 5 years old and felt unworthy and worthless, for no one taking you to the hospital when you swallowed a quarter, to the constant abuse you went through ... throughout your life. I am here with you, Louie, and you're very important to me. Thanks for coming out and playing "patty cake" last night. You make me laugh and have fun again. Thanks for being part of me. I'll write you all the time!

Dear Junior:

Hey there little dude ... I am here today to let you know I didn't forget about you – the little boy inside of me. I want to let you know I care and I am here for you. You've been in a corner of my mind and my heart since early childhood. I closed you away, so you wouldn't see the behaviors and actions that I put myself through, because of what happened to "us". I am here to tell you that what happened to you when you were 7 years old isn't your fault. You were an innocent little boy that didn't deserve to get boiling water thrown at you, just for losing the dice to the monopoly game. Though most of the water missed its' mark, it still burned and hurt and this event started your journey into the valley of unworthiness and the feeling that you couldn't do anything right and that everything was your fault. None of those thoughts were based on the boy you are. They were caused by an abusive parent who didn't know any better. I am here to let you know that not everyone in your life will be ignorant and abusive. Come out of that corner and we can do some of the things we didn't get a chance to do when you were little. Let's go play some catch with the football ... o.k.? I'll be writing you at least 2 o 3 times a week and we'll do something fun at the end each time, o.k.? Now, come on ... let's go play some catch ... I love you.   -Big Jr.

Hi Bear, it's me – Sara ... How are you? It sure has been a long time since I've heard from you. Me? I'm in this program trying to better myself and I want to build the relationship with you that I used to have. I'm really sorry I left you behind. I hope you'll be patient with me, so we can move on with our life, and I really need to take you with me. I love and miss you, Bear. I'll write again soon, o.k. ... Love you, Sara
8/21/06

Hi Billy ... it's me, William:

This is so hard for me to start. So much happened in your childhood. I haven't acknowledged you, deep in the recesses of my heart ... you've been acting out and I never caught it, until I came to treatment. I wanted to let you know that it wasn't your fault Dad left. Nothing you did, in this world, would have made him leave us ... it was just life. I know he never meant to make you feel it was your fault and I especially know that he never imagined Mom would start beating you because you looked like him. You endured being ignored, physically abused and neglected far too long. I blocked out all that when we were 17 and ran away and found a life of drugs and criminal behavior. The wrong people, places and things ... but I am here now and we will work through our feelings together. I am here to nurture you like you needed then. Why don't we go play on the swings at the park? You always liked that when Dad was around ... the park is just a short walk away. Let's go, buddy ... Love you, William

Summary – Damaged Emotions Chart

Here's your opportunity to express the clarity you've obtained from the Damaged Emotions Chart. Be *detailed* in addressing the Hurt, Belief, Goal, Behavior and Emotion, based on your chart. You'll be amazed at the freedom that self-awareness gives you.

_____
_____
_____
_____
_____
_____
_____
_____
_____
_____
_____
_____
_____
_____
_____
_____
_____
_____
_____
_____
_____
_____
_____
_____
_____
_____
_____
_____
_____
_____
_____
_____
_____

Adult Daily Affirmations

To achieve healing and change for the adult you've become, based on your childhood issues, also requires attention. You must destroy all those old messages, replacing them with positive reinforcement. This can be accomplished by giving yourself Daily Positive Affirmations. The inaccurate information given is a liability to your future success. Those messages are deep-rooted in your psyche and will emerge at any time. You must be prepared with a plan of action to disarm them.

Affirmation Progress:

1) Choose an affirmation* that will help you regain your power back, i.e., "I'm worthy today", "I can create a positive future", "I'm the matter that matters".

2) Look into your eyes in the mirror when you say it, otherwise saying it is useless. You must look into your soul (your eyes) to begin believing it. *(It will be uncomfortable at first, but you must persevere.)*

3) Start out by saying the Affirmation morning and night, as part of your meditation process. Also, say it anytime during the day or night, when your low self-esteem creeps in.

4) After you have come to believe ... choose another positive affirmation and repeat the same process.

*Saying adult affirmations at the same time as you nurture your child within allows "both" of you to integrate <u>one</u> strong, confident person, instead of being fragmented by the past.

Destination – Core Issue Chart

Core issues are the catalyst for most of our choices and decisions we make as adults. They are developed by many different situations where our basic needs were not met by our family of origin, or we were smothered by over-zealous caretakers who did not allow us to mature emotionally, spiritually or mentally. We must be aware of these core issues in order to honestly evaluate our present situations. When these issues go unchecked, we tend to <u>react</u> to situations, instead of responding to them in a healthy manner. This causes tension in *all* our relationships. The unresolved issues create emotional baggage, polluting any chance of making choices that aren't unconsciously motivated by them. In the next chapter, you are allowed to process, identify and grow through those issues in order to see the world and situations as they are and not distorted by past emotional baggage.

<u>GUIDE FOR CORE ISSUE CHART</u>

DISTORTED THINKING:

- Twisted perceptions which were manifested as a defense mechanism in order to cope with the chaos or dysfunctional environment you were subjected to.

CORE ISSUE: Central part of inmost part: the root

- Emotional abandonment:
  - Needs were not met mentally, i.e., nurturing, sensitivity, support guidance, protection, stability, etc.
- Physical abandonment:
  - Physically absent: unavailable for personal and physical bonding
- Molestation:
  - Physically violated whether it was fondling or actually sexual
- Physical Abuse/Violence:
  - Victim/witnessing domestic violence in household or being abused by someone on a regular basis.

PRESENTING ISSUES = ◯

- These are the coping skills you adopted as a result of events (usually negative), i.e., low self-worth, isolation, self-sabotage, etc.

NEGATIVE CONSEQUENCES = ▢

- These are the behaviors used to act out in an unhealthy and self-destructive way (usually subconsciously), i.e., rebellion, violence, denial, co-dependency

NOTE:

Do not add extra circles or squares to your core chart. If you do this, you will become overwhelmed because of the visual effect of seeing so many things wrong with you. As you continue the healing process, you will discover each issue integrates into each other anyway. This will allow you to heal naturally, without becoming overwhelmed.

You must also take the journey back to your childhood emotionally. This may be painful as you have probably buried these thoughts for years. In order for this process to ensure your self-awareness, you must mentally discover the "core" of your trauma, uncover the messages they gave you and discard the unconscious need to allow them to dictate your response to life situations today.

"DISTORTED THINKING"

Author's Chart

CORE ISSUES
1. **Emotional/Physical Abandonment**
2. **Molestation**
3. **Physical Abuse (Violence)**

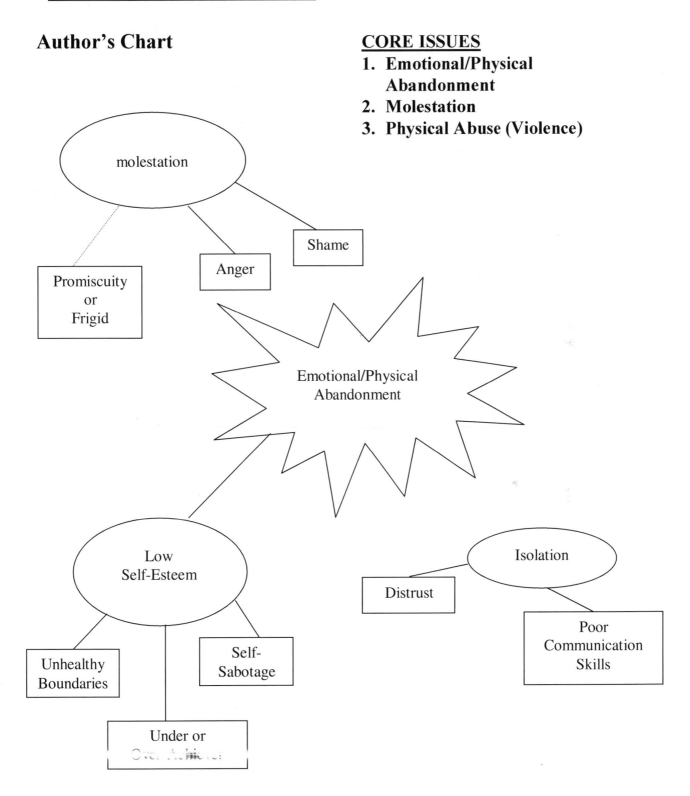

molestation

Shame

Anger

Promiscuity
or
Frigid

Emotional/Physical
Abandonment

Low
Self-Esteem

Isolation

Distrust

Unhealthy
Boundaries

Self-
Sabotage

Poor
Communication
Skills

Under or
Over Achiever

"DISTORTED THINKING"

EXAMPLE

CORE ISSUES
1. **Emotional/Physical Abandonment**
2. **Molestation**
3. **Physical Abuse (Violence)**

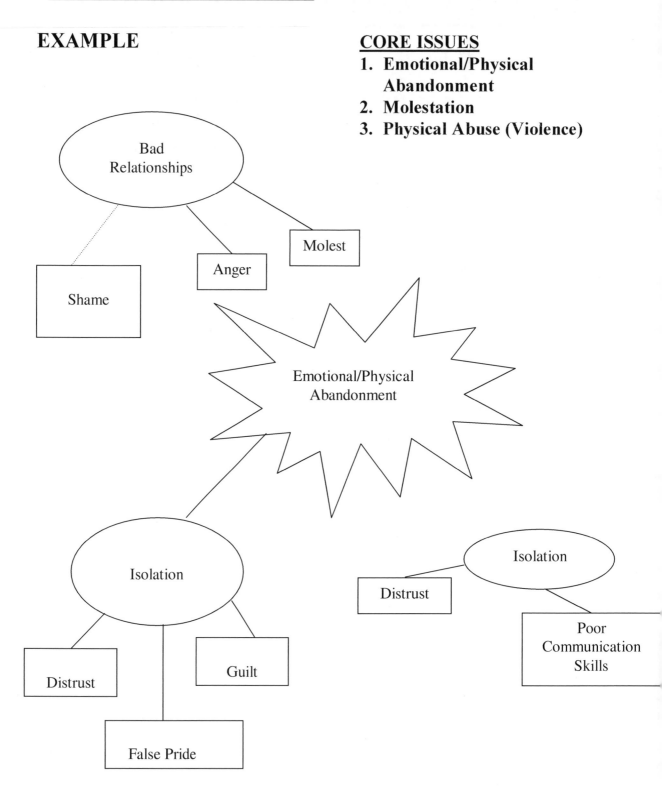

"DISTORTED THINKING"

EXAMPLE

CORE ISSUES
1. **Emotional/Physical Abandonment**
2. **Molestation**
3. **Physical Abuse (Violence)**

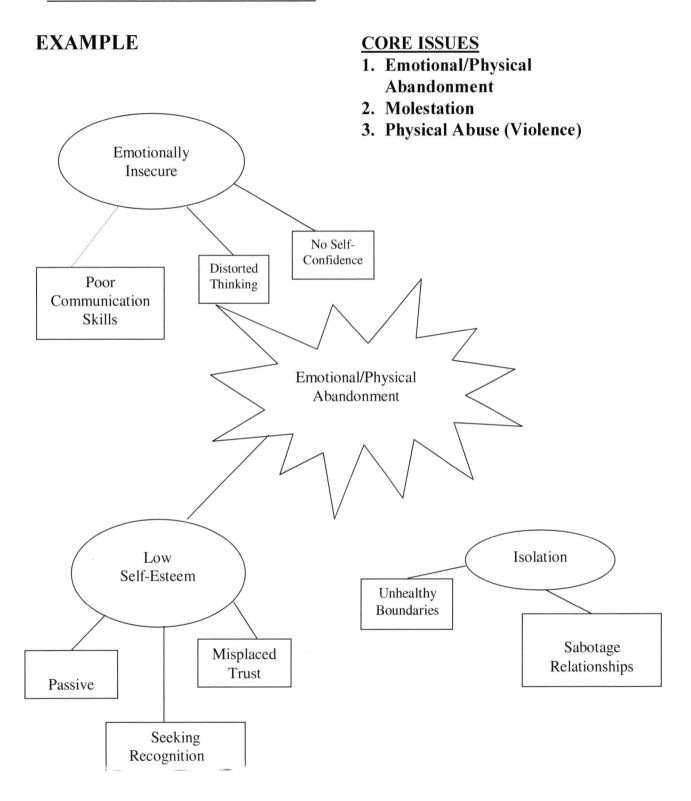

"DISTORTED THINKING"

EXAMPLE

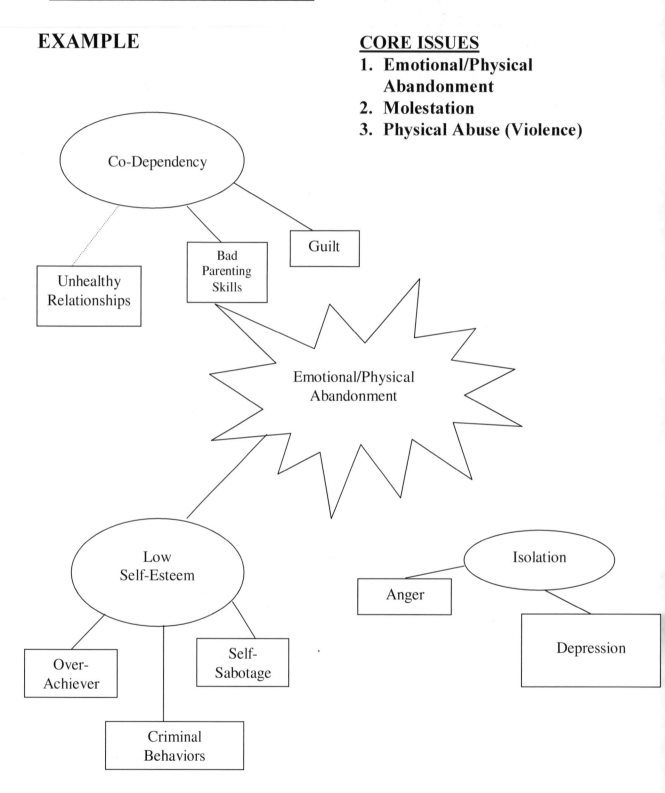

CORE ISSUES
1. **Emotional/Physical Abandonment**
2. **Molestation**
3. **Physical Abuse (Violence)**

Co-Dependency

Guilt

Unhealthy Relationships

Bad Parenting Skills

Emotional/Physical Abandonment

Low Self-Esteem

Isolation

Anger

Depression

Over-Achiever

Self-Sabotage

Criminal Behaviors

"DISTORTED THINKING"

YOUR CHART

CORE ISSUES
1. Emotional/Physical Abandonment
2. Molestation
3. Physical Abuse (Violence)

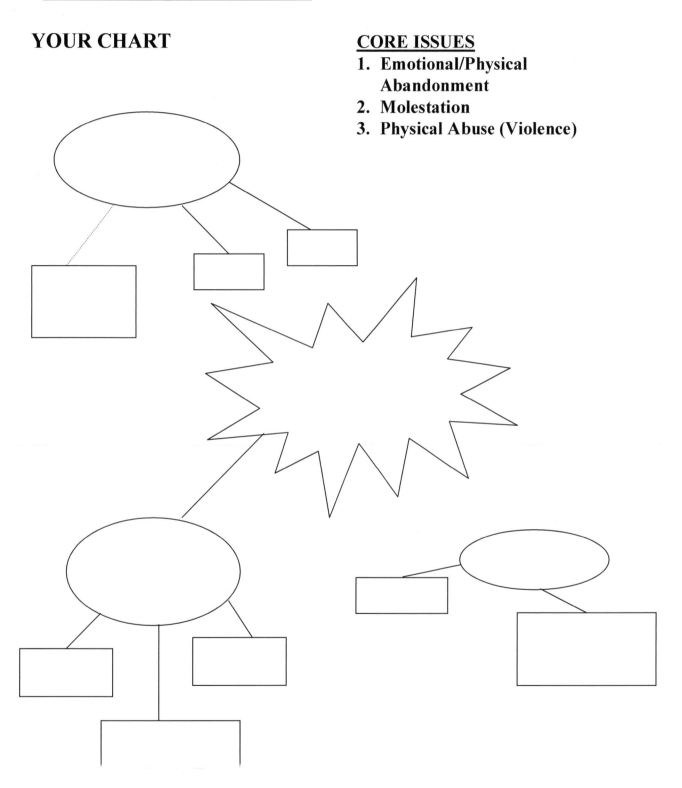

Achieving Closure After Core Chart

It's important to take the power from your past, of the inaccurate information that has dictated your reactions to people and situations. If the power isn't eradicated, all the messages you've uncovered will continue to control your responses negatively. Below are (2) examples of achieving closure and "freedom", based on where you are in your life.

Verbalizing Your Core Chart

Your empowerment comes from speaking the issues on your chart aloud. Each time you _connect_ a presenting issue or negative consequence to your "core" issue verbally, it becomes a reality and much more vivid. You see and feel why you are the person you've become. Find someone you trust and feel safe with to verbally process your Core Chart with. This should not be anyone your chart is about, for obvious reasons. It's about closure, not creating more hurtful situations.

If, in a treatment environment, this process should be done with a counselor, therapist, case manager, or group setting.

Chair Exercise

Now that you have verbalized your Core Chart, it's time to express emotionally, your pain, anger and hurt to the person you feel had the most significant role in your development into destruction, i.e., mom, dad, grandmother, perpetrator, etc. This will be your only chance to tell them how they have helped distort your choices in life. This process is very intense and should be done with someone emotionally strong that can absorb your anger as it's unleashed. Emotions will be overwhelming and powerful. You will be drained emotionally afterwards. The end result will be peace and a sense of relief. It's like a pressure cooker after you let out some of the steam.

*In a treatment setting, the client sits in a chair directly facing their counselor, therapist or case manager, who becomes the person responsible for the client's pain, anger and hurt. The client processes these emotions with no feedback from anyone. Their feelings must not be interrupted with anything that might detach them from expressing their emotional pain. After this process, a lot of positive affirmations and encouragement should follow the professional facilitating the process, as well as the client's peers.

SUMMARY OF CORE CHART*

Outline your core issue chart first, then the circumstances surrounding it. Then identify the circles (presenting issues) that stemmed from the "core issue" and how it created damaged emotions that you acquired to cope. Finally, outline the squares (negative consequences), which are the unhealthy behaviors acquired and carried into your life as an adult. The "Core Chart" is affectionately known, by clients, as a "firecracker".

Core Chart Summary:

_____
_____
_____
_____
_____
_____
_____
_____
_____
_____
_____
_____
_____
_____
_____
_____
_____
_____
_____
_____
_____
_____
_____
_____
_____
_____
_____
_____
_____
_____
_____
_____
_____

Destination ... Presenting Issue Process

You have identified a lot of dysfunctional behaviors resulting from your core issue chart, that requires a plan of action to ensure the cycle of self-destruction ends here. You must take one issue at a time and begin the healing process. Start with the issue that you feel caused the most havoc in your life. In most cases, it is low self-esteem. Your healing must start within or you will continue to go without the most important element of success ... YOU!

Directions: Identify each section with *events* and situations (in detail). Do not use just words in this space. The objective is for you to get a visual of where this Presenting Issue has taken you to. Simple words do not give you the opportunity to see the long-term effect the presenting issue has on you.

Presenting Issue: These are the circles on the core chart which you used as subconscious coping skills to endure the unwanted chaos occurring at the time, i.e., low self-esteem, anger, isolation, self-sabotage.

Negative Consequences: These are the squares on the Core Chart which you used to act out in an unhealthy way.
(Your frustrations, i.e., rebellion, violence, denial, co-dependency.)

Action Plan: These are things you can do to improve your behaviors in a positive way. Process and heal. This plan *must* be things you can DO, not just think about. Example: "I will affirm" myself in a positive way in the mirror daily, versus, "I will be a better person".

Aftercare Maintenance: These are the things you can DO daily to reinforce your goal to become "whole" again and reclaim a positive image of "self".

Presenting Issue: _____

_____
_____
_____
_____

Negative Consequences	**Action (Steps to Resolution)**
1)	1)
2)	2)
3)	3)

Aftercare Maintenance Plan:

_____
_____
_____
_____
_____
_____
_____
_____
_____
_____
_____
_____
_____
_____
_____
_____
_____
_____
_____
_____

Destination … Caretaker/Relationship Chart

It's very hard to form healthy relationships as an adult if you never experienced one growing up. What we see as a child molds our perceptions of what life is supposed to be (however distorted it is). We subconsciously repeat the same patterns, creating the same unhealthy results. Our primary caretakers are our role models and have a significant influence on our adult behaviors and choices. This segment will give you some answers as to why your relationships haven't been working

Directions for Caretaker/Relationship Chart

Caretakers (Mom/Dad) are the primary subjects of the first two boxes, whether or not they were emotionally available or physically present. We tend to discount the effect Mom/Dad played in our development. We block them out with our "wall of defense" saying, "It didn't bother me" or "not having them around didn't matter because grandma was great". Realistically, everyone needs and wants a mom and a dad.

The last box is for a significant person you had a history and relationship with. After filling in boxes with the appropriate responses, you will discover one of two things: (1) you pick one or both of your primary caretakers (whether they were there for you or not), or (2) you pick someone totally opposite from them and because of the messages you receive growing up, you misused their love and devotion not knowing what a healthy relationship was all about.

Caretaker/Relationship Chart

Fill in the boxes below by choosing three of your most important relationships. Fill in each box by telling what you wanted in the relationship (time, attention, affection, etc.), then what you really got, what the status of the relationship is now (how you interact or how the relationship ended), how you felt when it ended or how you feel now about the relationship if it is still intact.

NAME:			
EMOTIONAL NEEDS	LOVE, SUPPORT, GUIDANCE, NURTURING* EVERYONE WANTS THESE THINGS	LOVE, SUPPORT, GUIDANCE, NURTURING	LOVE, SUPPORT, GUIDANCE, NURTURING
DISAPPOINTMENTS IN RELATIONSHIPS			
OUTCOME & DISALLUSIONMENT			
EMOTIONAL BAGGAGE OR TRAUMA			

Summary of Caretaker/Relationship Chart (What Did You Discover?) ...

Destination ... Relationship Inventory

Here is your opportunity to see how the "hurts" uncovered by your damaged emotion chart and the "issues" outlined in your core chart has transcended in your intimate relationships, sabotaging them. Hopefully, after referring to your "Relationship Chart", you can identify a pattern similar to your primary caretaker's as well. You will get a clear picture of the behaviors you projected in each relationship, destroying a chance for a happy, healthy ending.

Relationship Inventory – (2) Examples

Example 1

Name: _____ **Relationship:** _____

Intentions for entering the relationship:

_____
_____
_____
_____
_____
_____

Behavior during the relationship:

_____
_____
_____
_____
_____
_____
_____

Issues that surfaced in the relationship:

_____
_____
_____
_____
_____

End result of relationship:

_____
_____
_____
_____
_____

Take this opportunity to review your answers to the relationship inventory exercise. Use the space below to examine "your part" in the ultimate collapse of the relationship. You must identify areas in *detail* and with total *honesty* of: suspicion, bitterness, dishonesty, selfishness, jealousy, and your lack of consideration. Remember to stay focused only on "your part". After you've completed this part, write out how you could have handled these situations differently.

Summary of Relationship Inventory

Destination ... Internal Forgiveness

You have discovered the hurt which set the stage for your core issues, influencing everything you've done thus far. You have probably uncovered a lot of unresolved emotions, causing some guilt. Your guilt/shame is a result of you taking ownership of situations that were pre-destined by your core issues. Most of these events were completely out of your control and internal forgiveness for "self" is your first order of business. In this next session, you will have the opportunity to process those feelings of guilt/shame and move forward through to internal forgiveness.

Three Stages for Internal Forgiveness

1) **Owning Your Part by Releasing Denial:** Admit what you've done and how your self-centeredness and distorted thinking has affected those you care about and how you feel without blaming others for anything. Also, acquire the humility to make the necessary amends.

2) **Experiencing a Paradigm Shift in Order to Focus on the Lesson:** Be kind to yourself! Stop beating yourself up for choices made, but be honest in your willingness to be accountable for your actions without any excuses. Examine the emotions that emerged from each experience, reinforcing your powerlessness, shame and misplaced self-loathing.

3) **Allow Yourself Emotional Healing Through Positive Support and Guidance:**

Seeking help from those genuinely concerned with supporting you through healing beyond the trauma. Find a safe environment to process negative experiences, i.e., counselors, clergy and support groups designed to assist you with positive reinforcements. This enables you to rebuild your self-esteem, which allows the healing to begin.

Write out how you can apply each of the (3) Stages for Internal Forgiveness to achieve the healing to become "whole" again.

1) Owning your part by releasing denial:

_____

_____

_____

_____

_____

_____

_____

_____

2) Experiencing a paradigm shift in order to focus on the lesson:

_____

_____

_____

_____

_____

_____

_____

_____

_____

3) Allow yourself emotional healing through positive support/guidance:

_____

_____

_____

_____

_____

_____

_____

_____

_____

PART III

After The Pain

(Discovering a New You)

Table of Contents

Part III 'After the Pain'

Page

Introduction

Discovering a New You

Looking for the good "inside you" after "uncovering the truth" outlined in previous chapters is an essential part of reaching your destiny and full potential. This destination is his final installment in balancing all the information absorbed so far. What positive legacies have you derived from your childhood and adolescence? What positive survival skills have emerged from your struggles to cope? How can you begin to re-channel the distorted thinking that has caused you to react to situations rather than respond? You must experience a complete "paradigm shift*" or psyche change to fully acknowledge all that is good in you. These gifts have gone unnoticed for far too many years. In this chapter, you will be given the necessary tools required to identify your true value, gifts and purpose. Embrace this opportunity and use your past as a spring board to a new you.

*Paradigm Shift – A perception or opinion that changes position or direction.

Stage I – Identifying Your Potential

First you must create a mission statement on paper. This will allow you to have a mental and visual reference point. Your mission statement is the foundation in building your dreams for the future. It also enables you to remain focused during those times you may become distracted from your ultimate goal.

(3) Components are required for a mission statement:

A) **Purpose** – Your divine calling to make a difference; something you feel passionate about.

B) **Vision** – A vivid picture or a premonition of what you want to achieve based on your divine purpose – the end result of fulfilling your passion.

C) **Goal** – What future accomplishment will be achieved to secure your purpose in making a difference; what is your legacy left, based on your vision.

Your Divine Plan or Mission Statement

Purpose:

_____
_____
_____
_____
_____
_____

Vision:

_____
_____
_____
_____
_____
_____

Goal:

_____
_____
_____
_____
_____
_____

It's important to have a way to gauge your mission statement. This is done by creating short and long term goals, which can be used to monitor your progress.

Short term – Allows you to put a plan in place with small steps of careful preparation to obtain your goal. This allows you to measure your progress and avoid becoming overwhelmed or giving up, due to discouragement. These goals must be precise to keep you focused. Your short term goals:

_____
_____
_____
_____
_____

Long-term goals – allow you to visualize your success on paper before they materialize. This adds the much needed motivation to continue moving forward. Again, be _precise_ in what you want to accomplish. Your long term goals:

_____
_____
_____
_____
_____

*Avoid self-sabotage (know the difference)

Confidence vs. Ego

Confidence: Self-assurance, positive self-worth, empowered.
Ego: Over-zealous self-worth, distorted by your perception of yourself or situations.

The danger with having too much ego and not enough confidence can be devastating to your success. Ego blocks out any guidance or direction by the divine spirit. The spirit can't get in because your ego tells you "I got this under control". The divine spirit doesn't argue with your ego. It will wait patiently until you surrender or lose everything. Remember, ego will always **Edge God Out**!

Identify a time your ego blocked your success:

_____
_____
_____
_____
_____
_____
_____

D) Multiply what is fruitful in you; when we attempt to reach a goal, we are full of doubts based on our past failures. Because of this subconscious thought process, we often fail. Take this time to itemize those natural abilities you already have. These are called "seeds of talent". By doing this, you are able to see the gifts of success are in *YOU*. Your Seeds of Talent:

_____	_____
_____	_____
_____	_____

*Don't multiply failures in your life, but identify your success and repeat them.

Stage II – Minimize Liabilities

Obstacles will enter your life causing you to lose focus and direction. People, places and situations often deter us from succeeding in life. Sometimes these deterrents of defeat come fast, leading to powerful consequences. On other occasions, they are slow, cunning and very methodical. The destruction left behind can be devastating. If we don't stay focused on the prize, failure is inevitable. Use this opportunity to identify these liabilities that are already in place, and those lurking to defeat you in the future.
Liabilities:

_____	_____
_____	_____
_____	_____

Stage III – Don't Waste Time

The most important question you can ask yourself is "What am I going to do with the time I have left?" There will be a lot of distractions on the way to accomplishing your mission statement. Watch out for these distractions. Be mindful and ask yourself "Will doing this take me off track?" If the answer is yes … don't do it!! Remember time is a valuable commodity that we often take for granted and realize it after it's too late.

Identify a situation where distraction reaped a negative outcome:

_____
_____
_____
_____
_____
_____
_____
_____
_____
_____
_____

Stage IV – Maintenance Plan

It's not enough to create a mental plan for your dreams or even by putting that plan on paper. You <u>must</u> continuously work on improvement by nurturing that plan with extra attention. For anything in life to reach its' maximum potential, maintenance is essential, i.e., plants, children, pets, cars, lawn, clothes ... Everything! Your mission statement is no exception. Any task half done can only reap half the success. Go back to your mission statement and write your maintenance plan needed to experience success. This should include things you can do on a daily or weekly basis to nurture your dream for the future.

Maintenance Plan:

_____

_____

_____

_____

_____

_____

_____

_____

_____

Stage V – Market Your Success

There are things you can do to enhance your assets in order to attract success. Your compassion in expressing your mission is probably the most important thing you can do and this comes naturally because _you_ believe! There are some things you do outwardly to market success, i.e., clothes, speech, friends, etc. These are all a part of your table of contents, much like a book providing a guide for what's inside it. Create your personal table of contents below:

_____   _____

_____   _____

_____   _____

_____   _____

_____   _____

_____   _____

Stage VI – Merge Your Assets

Every dream needs a team of like-minded people to become a reality. Surround yourself with those who compliment and also encourage your vision of success. We often attract who we are, so be mindful of the energy you transmit. Celebrating the smallest of successes in accomplishing your mission statement will renew the creative potential in you to excel. Don't go where you're merely tolerated. Go where you are celebrated instead! List some people who could be valuable team players:

_____   _____

_____   _____

_____   _____

_____   _____

_____   _____

Stage VII – Manage the Opportunity When Presented

Things will happen that take you back or throw you off course. Staying focused is the key to fulfilling your goals even when a curve ball is thrown in your court. You must learn how to regroup after a setback, by automatically preparing for a comeback. Use the space below to identify the 3 C's in situations that reaped negative consequences in your life.

1) **CONFESS** – Admit you may have blown it by miscalculating your position. Acknowledge your mistake without beating yourself up.
   Remember, "Don't Waste Time".

   _____
   _____
   _____
   _____
   _____
   _____

2) **CORRECT** – Re-examine your areas of defeat with a new plan. It's always good to have at least (2) alternate plans in place so the air isn't knocked out of you when the first plan fails … you have a back-up.

   _____
   _____
   _____
   _____
   _____
   _____

3) **CREATE** – Start now by always rebuilding the opportunity lost and embrace a stronger vision of success. Examine the flaws in your plan that failed and see what you can do to improve it. Remember all the qualities you've identified previously … now is the time to apply them!

*Adversity will always motivate you to move past the confusion and devastation of defeat. These challenges create character and the tenacity to succeed.

10 Steps to "A New You" Summary

1) **Pray for a vision:** Make sure you are connected to your inner self or "spirit" self. God must have a healthy vessel to transmit His plan through you.

2) **Live within your means:** Put a budget in place and stick to it. Learning to manage your finances is essential. Once your vision and purpose are realized, don't buy that outfit just because it looks good ... remember your life has another purpose.

3) **Play:** We become so enmeshed in success and reaching our goals, we forget to enjoy life. Replenish your spirit while keeping your eyes on the prize.

4) **Go where you're celebrated, not tolerated:** You will encounter those people who are jealous of your vision and your zest to enjoy life. Avoid negativity at all costs! Don't allow anyone to steal your joy of who you are.

5) **Learn to say "NO":** Being focused and spiritually sound helps you to set boundaries about what you will and will not accept. Remember NO means NO ... be FIRM, with conviction.

6) **Don't waste time:** A lot of life experiences have stifled your productivity up until now. Reclaim your place at the top. There's no more time to complain about what could have been. Make a plan and do the necessary footwork to accomplish it.

7) **Change the view:** Be flexible with your perceptions. Tolerance is the gateway to compassion and compassion starts with self.

8) **Work on your challenges:** Obstacles offer you a chance to grow and realize how strong you really are. Tackle your challenges one at a time to obtain clarity and empowerment.

9) **Understand your strength:** Know what you're good at and multiply them with daily practice. Your destiny was pre-ordained and everything required to achieve it lies within you already.

10) **Learn from your mistakes:** Don't become stagnant by your mistakes. Use them as lessons to get it right the next time. Without mistakes, there can't be experience to help yourself or others in the future.

INTO ACTION ... YOUR COMMITMENT TO CHANGE

Below is an "action" list of positive activities/behaviors you are willing to start. This enables you to make a *serious* commitment to successful change. To complete this process, there is a space to list some attitudes/behaviors you will need to discontinue in order to destroy your future of failure.

*Be honest and thorough with your commitments!

I will start ...	I will stop ...
1)	1)
2)	2)
3)	3)
4)	4)
5)	5)

Signature: _____ Date: _____

You have discovered many outstanding qualities if you have done a thorough job in the preceding pages. Now, it's time to write out the "new you", based on the information you learned. Review each section and use the gifts and talents you have identified in the space below. This is *your* reminder of who you have become.

_____
_____
_____
_____
_____
_____
_____
_____
_____
_____
_____
_____
_____
_____
_____
_____
_____
_____
_____
_____
_____
_____
_____
_____
_____
_____
_____
_____
_____
_____
_____
_____

** Behold the essence of greatness! **

Final Destination ... Alumni Revelations

"I never would have admitted that the actions of my adult life came from the pain and hurt of my past. According to me, there was never any pain and hurt. My whole life was a false sense of independence, not needing or wanting anything and not really 'feeling' much of anything good, bad or indifferent."

"'Family Dynamics' was amazing to me. It helped me to see why I act the way I do, and the bottom line is that most of my life has been based on fear. Fear of you, fear of me and fear of rejection. I would never let anyone in, because no one would ever do anything but hurt me. I drank and used to cover up my feelings, to have courage and that false sense of 'independence'. Take that away and I was weak, vulnerable and scared. By uncovering my past and learning to accept it, it has opened doors for me I never could have imagined. I learned that emotional abandonment is my core issue. I never was important or good enough and that made me reject and fear me and you."

"Doing the work and learning how to forgive and love them, no matter what, has been the greatest gift anyone has ever given me. I have learned that although I am never responsible for the actions of others; I am 100% responsible for my reaction and what I do with my feelings. I have the most wonderful relationship with my family. I may not always love what they do, but I'll always love them. Most important, I love myself and I am enough. I have become truly independent. I have my own house, car and I just got a job in a recovery center doing something that I love ... by giving back."

"Although I am very active in AA and NA, I believe the beginning of our journey sets the stage for it all. Without the work I have done in 'Family Dynamics' I'm not sure where I'd be or how I'd feel about it. I have my heart back!"

Robin M.   2006

"My name is Deanna and I am a 47 year old woman who has served 5 prison terms on separate CDC numbers. Not proud. Just a fact. I became an addict at a young age. When I first was told I was eligible to go to DTF, I said 'Cool, anything is better than Chowchilla'. So, my journey began. I arrived at the DTF in June, 2006 and was angry and scared and said 'Send me back to prison'. I didn't want to do the work it would take to get through the program. I thought wt was going to be easy. You see, I'm a 'thinker'. I'm always trying to think of an easier, softer way. Trying to figure things out and do things *my own way*. I wanted to do as little work as possible and slide right through the program, but after about a week of being there, I was perceived as unapproachable and intimidating. Perhaps I preferred myself that way. I had spent the better part of my adult life in and out of jail or prison and I am a quick-witted person who manipulated people all my life, so I did not like the focus on me. Sure, focus on YOU. I'm real good at focusing on others and accurate at calling you on what you need. I got smashed real quick when I was put in a class called 'Family Dynamics'. My whole world crushed in an instant! All my fantasy and denial, Bam! I was a happy, well-adjusted child, you see. That's crap. I was abandoned at age 4 and learned to use and manipulate men to get my needs met emotionally because I had low self-esteem and that set me up to be raped. That triggered off so much criminal thinking, it's unbelievable. Man, you won't believe how free I am today, after re-parenting y little girl through all of that pain and putting blame where it needed to be buried and just let it GO!! I don't hold onto all that guilt and shame anymore and I have moved on with my life and I am a productive member of society that has a healthy relationship with my children and God. I work at a job that values me as an employee. I manage over 200 people. My parole officer calls me when my company hires one of his parolees and asks about the person or even to just say 'Hi'. I'm accountable. Today, I can honestly say I don't see prison as a part of my future, except to go back as a panel to speak and give HOPE! 'Family Dynamics' has altered the course of my life."

Eternally Grateful Deanna   2006

I was a complete mess, lost in my own skin and completely lost from reality … 34 years old and I thought there was no hope for me, but after going through the 'Family Dynamics' class and experiencing the core chart, I found that there is hope for a person like me. I was able to talk through my life as a child, to the adult I am today, understanding why my life was the way it was. It was so simple, I couldn't believe it. Wow!"

"I'm not saying it was easy (emotionally). It was one of the most humbling experiences in my life, but after experiencing this, the whole concept was now very clear with this new understanding I had. I am now able to walk through each day of my life with a new found hope for my life and for my children. This is because I see through a new set of eyes. When I left from the program in February, 2007, I had no choice but to take this information with me."

"It's been 14 months since I left that program and it's kind of funny how life works, because everything in my life is so different and nothing has really changed. Just the way I see my life. The world is still the same, my family is still the same, and life is still the same. I have been drug-free for 23 months and dealing with my family on a daily basis, along with everyday life's ups and downs. I am able to do this because of what I learned from 'Family Dynamics'. It's so powerful … just amazing. My life is so precious and full of meaning. I am just so grateful for this new understanding I have and blessed to know that 'Family Dynamics' is for the rest of my life."

Sheila J.   2006

"Hello, my name is Crystal. I'm 30 years old and I have 5 children. Let me tell you a little bit about me. My life growing up was hard. I had loving parents, but there were a lot of secrets and a lot of fighting. My life was dysfunctional. Like many others, I became a drug addict. I started my criminal behavior and was in and out of jails and prisons, losing my children … my life had fallen apart. I got comfortable doing time so that's what I did – lots of time. I gave up on myself until this last time. I met a lady that believed in me, that showed me how to learn, to work through my life and today, my life is beyond my wildest dreams. I will discharge parole this month, which is amazing for me. I have a full-time job. I am buying my home and I own my own vehicle. My children are moving back home in June and I am, for the first time, having a normal relationship. I'm about to get married and can you really believe I am in school for drug and alcohol counseling. I am really living life on life's terms and I love it. I enjoy my life today. Thank you for everything."

Crystal   2006

"This was me in the beginning … I was reserved, didn't like to put too much of my business out to my peers or counselors. I definitely had my guard up. I didn't show much emotion because I was blind to what was inside. While I was there, I started to identify with things I had no clue about. I became aware of what my core issues were. Number one being the 'Lost Child'. I was the victim of rape and domestic violence numerous times, which of course, led me to my disease. I was the bottle stuffed to the top, also losing a loved one whom I never dealt with. I was always numbing my emotions. How the chart helped me was that once I learned to speak on these issues and told my story, it was a huge burden lifted from me. It was not only a spiritual awakening, but a 'rebirth of me', or as my counselor put it – the 'transformation of the butterfly'. Today, I am an independent, working woman who is working her way up to the top. I have successfully discharged parole and I have 2 years clean. I have contact with my children and they are back in my life. I have a job. I am a functional person now. I can walk with my head up today. I am free."

Linda C.   2006

Today

Today, I thank God for the air I breathe;

Praying that my self-doubt be relieved.

Be instilled with courage to live productively;

Accepting who I am not, but who I'd like to be.

Growing from mistakes that won't go away;

Making the best of situations,

I'll start "Today".

In closing … I hope this journey has given you the wisdom and courage to write the next chapter of your life. This will require a commitment from you to do the work. You have the tools to conquer those negative experiences of the past. Create more meaningful relationships and empower yourself using the gifts you've discovered. Your destiny was pre-ordained. Be willing to make and accept change. With a renewed spirit that paves the way, it's time to reach for the stars … and catch them!

"God Bless"

Personal Notes and References

Personal Notes and References

Personal Notes and References

Personal Notes and References

Personal Notes and References

Personal Notes and References